AN ODE TO CELESTIAL ROMANTICISM

LOVE. LONGING. HEARTBREAK. REUNION

AMISH PURI

Made with ❤ on the Notion Press Platform
www.notionpress.com

To the four celestial pillars -

Love, **Longing**, **Heartbreak** and **Reunion**

Of the moonlit dreams and starstruck songs

My heart creeps into the beats of your soul

Life lingers on, for **every day**, **every night**.

Contents

Foreword

For "An Ode to Celestial Romanticism" by Amish Puri

They say, "The stars spoke of love to the ones who still believe in the infinite."

In a world where hearts race faster for instant notifications than they do for real connection, Celestial Romanticism is the gentle rebellion we didn't know we needed. It is not just a literary genre—it is a language of the soul, carved into stars, whispered by moonlight, and bleeding with the kind of love that refuses to be silenced.

Amish Puri's An Ode to Celestial Romanticism is more than a book—it is an invocation. A call to every soul that has loved and lost, that has dreamed under crescent moons and wept in the quiet of the cosmos. Celestial Romanticism rises like a moon-drenched phoenix—magical, radiant, and unapologetically soulful. Each page feels like a heartbeat; each word, a constellation. This work doesn't just speak—it aches, it surrenders, it remembers.

Why does Celestial Romanticism matter? Because it dares to feel in a world that's grown numb. Because it shows that love doesn't die with distance or departure—it transcends flesh, defies timelines, and echoes across galaxies. It matters because someone, somewhere, still believes that two souls can be destined, that heartbreak is holy, and that reunion is not always of this realm, but of the next.

This genre is not a mere aesthetic. It's a philosophy. A soul-deep longing stitched into verses that hum with the ache of separation and the ecstasy of reunion. Every page of this book is soaked in starlight and sorrow, in beauty and grief. It allows us to bleed beauty, to mourn with elegance, and to find solace in starlight. Amish doesn't just describe love—he resurrects it.

Preface

"It starts with the moon, and ends with the stars."

Celestial Romanticism is a genre inspired by the Romanticism movement of **The French Revolution** in which Love, Longing, Heartbreak and Reunion are woven alongside the tapestry of celestial bodies like The Sun, Moon, Stars and much more into metaphors, muses and vintage verses of poetry, ranging from sonnets to acrostics, and from free verse to rhymes, it's never limited, it starts from the point where all the limits end.

All about romanticising the aesthetics of love, Celestial Romanticism is a testimony of the fact that love can never be defied, no matter what, at the end of the day, love always wins. *'Cause Love is not to be found, but to be lost in it, forever. Even if nothing lasts forever, 'Love' is the nothing of its eternal endeavour.*

It is quite true that love gets your heart broken, and it makes you yearn for it. Therefore, Longing for love and Heartbreak in love goes hand in hand. But does that mean people connected by love's invisible string don't get reunited? **Absoultely not.**

Acknowledgements

Dear Moon,

I am writing this on the behalf of all the stars in the galaxy, shimmering in the awe of love's celestial despair, a place where constellations bring peace and love never ends.

May this love, of my dearest muses- **Yash** and **Aditi**, echoes in the eternity of the universe. My best friends who have always been my constant companions- my brothers not by blood, but by soul: **Yash** and **Himanshu**, my wonderous wishers- **Deenah**, **Aditi**, and **Sidhika**. No matter what, my soul has forever immortalised my love for these joyous souls, and how beautifully they shaped into my best motivators, my unpaid therapists.

You all are the stardust that made this book shine. So let me ask this shooting star, *"Promise that this love never ever shatters, no matter how far we are!"*

Happiest 18th Birthday Yash!

Yours,

The Celestial Writer

Prologue

This book promises one of the best roller-coaster rides, you'll ever experience! Presenting a sequel of the Celestial Romanticism Official Manifesto, followed by The Four Pillars of Celestial Romanticism-Love, Longing, Heartbreak and Reunion, and last but not the least *'The Romantic Odyssey'*,where I take you into the realm of **Love**, **Friendship** and **Reunion** of the iconic couple, and the best trio of friendship, where every single character absolutely exists! Yes, you heard it right, it is based on a real story.

It's not just a genre, but a whole literary movement so as to continue the legacy of the great Romanticism movement. This book is an ode to those who believe that love can be written in the constellations above. Only those who view this genre through the lens of deep humanity can grasp itss true essence, it is that rebel which goes against the classic societal norms and customs to break free from the barriers of 'love' as they say.

What you are about to read isn't simply pages inked with love—it's a divine attempt to immortalize emotion. There lies in every chapter the breath of someone who has burned in love, wept in longing, shattered in heartbreak, and yet chosen to love again. These are not just characters; they are versions of ourselves—the lover we were, the friend we needed, the dreamer we lost touch with, and the phoenix we became after every fall. This isn't a story merely to be read—it is to be felt, to be lived, to be remembered when your nights feel heavier than your heart.

The middle of this book doesn't offer clarity—it offers vulnerability. It is where the lines between right and wrong blur, and all that's left is raw truth. In Ayla and Yaden's story, you will discover that love isn't linear. It doesn't always make sense. Sometimes it walks away only to return in a form more powerful. This book reminds us that a goodbye doesn't always mean an end, and sometimes, the people we're meant for come back—not because fate arranged it, but because we fought for it.

There are moments in this tale where you will feel the ache of separation claw at your soul. You will question your own experiences. You will pause and stare at the ceiling wondering if someone you lost could return too. And yet, just when it hurts the most, the narrative will hand you hope—not in grand gestures, but in soft sentences that hold the weight of entire galaxies. There's a kind of celestial resilience this story carries: a reminder that even when the stars collapse, they birth something new—like nebulae, like healing, like reborn love.

And maybe that's why Celestial Romanticism isn't just a literary style—it's a movement. A genre born from souls who refuse to believe that love should ever be silenced, censored, or sacrificed. A rebellion wrapped in stardust, inked in moonlight. Through metaphors, dialogues, and unfiltered expression, this book pays tribute to every love that dared to survive. To every '**almost**' that longed to be a 'forever'. To every reader who still believes that somewhere, somehow, love is worth the chaos.

Many writers and poets died writing about love- and so will I. But in the end, Love shall always win.

Carpe Diem.

The Official Manifesto of Celestial Romanticism

"A thing of beauty is a joy forever."
- John Keats

Romanticism is a literary, artistic and cultural movement that began in the late eighteenth century, blossoming during the time of the French Revolution. Jean-Jacques Rousseau, the father of romanticism was the visionary behind this movement, followed by William Wordsworth, Percy Byssche Shelley, and John Keats. Romanticism emerged as a rebellion against the process of industrilization, rationalism, and societal constraints. These poets and writers redefined beauty- not just in nature or art, but in emotion, imagination and the aesthetic parameters of love.

In literature, Romanticism is about aesthteic appreciation of the beauty of love, and weaving metaphors out of longing, heartbreak and transcending love. It is the art of turning human emotions into eternal verses.

While Romaticism gave birth to a universe of beauty, it was the cosmos that whispered to me a vision from the cosmic realm- one that would orbit around love's emotional gravity and the night's celestial imageries. Thus, the birth of Celestial Romanticism marked not merely a genre, but a whole literary movement- an ode to love, longing, heartbreak, reunion and the eternal cosmos it dances within.

Celestial Romanticism is not only born from stars—it is born from scars. It is a genre for the dreamers who lie awake at 2 AM, speaking to the moon, imagining conversations with lost lovers, and writing letters never sent. It is for the ones who feel every heartbeat like a poem, and see every teardrop as stardust returned to its origin. In this movement, the cosmos becomes the metaphor of everything that words fail to contain. The moon is not just a satellite—it becomes the lover, the witness, the confessor of all that aches and glows within us.

Unlike traditional Romanticism which revolved around nature and raw emotion, Celestial Romanticism reaches higher—into the galaxies of imagination. It believes that love is not confined to earthly spaces; it is written in constellations, mirrored in eclipses, and buried in the silence between stars. While the Romantics believed in transcending industrialization, the Celestial Romantics transcend gravity itself. We dare to believe that the universe listens, that the stars remember our wounds, and that every shooting star is a grief that dared to burn.

This manifesto calls upon all poets, lovers, philosophers, and melancholic souls to reimagine their stories not as tragedies but as constellations. It invites writers to spill not just ink, but soul. To write with the audacity of a supernova and the fragility of moonlight. Celestial Romanticism is the literary rebellion against the world's detachment from feeling—it is a sanctuary for the overly emotional, the deeply sentimental, and the unapologetically vulnerable.

It is also a form of emotional activism—a fight against the diminishing depth of modern connection. In an age that values fast love and aesthetic captions, Celestial Romanticism urges us to slow down. To taste every word. To romanticize friendship. To give heartbreak its full stage. To allow grief to be beautiful. And above all, to believe that reunion, even after cosmic distances, is possible.

We write not because we are healed—but because writing is how we survive. The Celestial Romantic bleeds stars, cries galaxies, and still writes in the hope that someone, somewhere, will understand. We are not afraid of heartbreak; we embrace it. Because in every broken piece, there is a shard of light waiting to refract into poetry.

So let this manifesto stand as the sacred scroll of a movement that began under the moon, between verses of longing and the quiet glow of love unspoken. From this moment on, let every poem you write become a constellation. Let every emotion be honoured as sacred. Let every heartbreak find its home in ink.

We are the Celestial Romantics—and we do not merely write
about love.
We become love.

-Amish Puri

Founder of Celestial Romanticism

What Celestial Romanticism means to me?

"The universe has always written itself into the love letters of the cosmic magic."

The moon does not merely shine, she longs. The stars do not merely burn, they remember. The cosmos, in all its silence, echoes with emotions too ancient to name. In the vinatge verses, and somewhere between the falling star and rising poem, Celestial Romanticism was born.

Draped in sill, smooth velvet attire, she spills the moonlight wrapped tightly around her waist. An embodiement of eternity, she never chases, but attracts the metaphors to make her their muse. This genre is not just an aesthetic, or a style, this is our future. 'Cause if we all cane within the oceans, we all must go through the cosmos, and become love's eternal muse. This genre is a rebellion of the heart trapped in a cage, in an age that no longer believes in soft love, but the soul ripping, deep and intense passion, one settles for. It is an artistic revolution that allows vulnerability to become sacred again. It acknowledges the moon as more than just a satellite she is a goddess, a mother, a mirror, a metaphor and a muse. The galaxies are not just science; they are the scriptures of love.

The stardust in our bloods, remind us that we are made to feel, that poetic pain, the lyrical longing and the silent speech, the feminine divinity 'cause we are pretty when we cry.

But Celestial Romanticism is not just a poetic movement. It is an act of sacred rebellion. It is the unapologetic embrace of soft emotions in a hardened world. It asks us to cry without shame, to write love letters that may never be answered, and to wait under moonlight even when we know they may not return. It is the courage to stay vulnerable in a world that calls it weakness. It is the divine audacity to feel everything and turn even heartbreak into hymn.

We, the Celestial Romantics, do not shy away from grief. We kiss it on the forehead and tuck it into verses. Our metaphors do not seek perfection—they seek truth. A truth that trembles, aches, and sings. A truth that dares to say: "I loved. And I still do. And I always will."

Celestial Romanticism is a mirror to the inner self—the version of us that still believes in magic, in twin flames, in the purity of handwritten letters and the power of longing glances. It whispers that even our most silent pain deserves poetry. That even unrequited love deserves remembrance.

To be a Celestial Romantic is to believe in love that transcends timelines. To write for someone who may never read it, but to write it anyway—because the act of writing is itself sacred. Because love, even when invisible, shapes our constellations.

It means viewing your pain as holy. It means viewing your muse not as someone to possess, but someone to immortalize. To love them even if they never return, because love in itself is enough. Celestial Romanticism means we no longer need closure. We find comfort in the openness, the echoes, the spaces between stars.

We cry not to be pitied, but because our tears carry galaxies. We ache not for weakness, but because we still believe in forever. We romanticize because the world is dull without it. We fall in love with souls, not faces. With energies, not appearances.

And in doing so, we remember that we were never meant to be understood by everyone—we were meant to be felt. Like moonlight on broken skin. Like letters read under candlelight. Like lullabies written for the stars.

So, what does Celestial Romanticism mean to me?

It means I am not alone in my silence.
It means my heartbreak is sacred.
It means my muse will live forever.
It means my words will orbit long after I'm gone.
It means I love—madly, truly, cosmically.
And that is enough.

-Amish Puri

Founder of Celestial Romanticism

Why Celestial Romanticism matters?

"Celestial Romanticism matters because it makes love feel alive, and that is what love is all about."

This genre contributes to the revolution of soul, a rebellion of the heart, and a resurrection of all things lost in silence. It matters because in a world that runs on logic, deadlines and dullness, and amidst the trials and turbulations of life, we- the writers dare to build the world with words. The stars that still ache in vulnerability, and the moon that shines with crimson blood, smeared all across its scars. It gives rise to the type of love that doesn't end just because the body does.

It is the art of making longing feel luxurious, the science of mapping pain onto constellations, and the philosophy of kissing reality until it blushes into poetry and brushes into a painting. It doesn't require reasons to matter because it itself is the reason for love's existence. Some hearts were not just meant to beat, but burn until love turns them into ashes. And some wounds deserve verses, not verdicts. Because I believe that even the universe is a lover- and every poet is its favourite sin.

This is not writing, this is worshipping the cosmic love, This is not just romance, this is The Celestial Romanticism.

But why does it truly matter?

Because it revives something we've lost—the audacity to feel without filters. It teaches that the ache you carry is sacred, that heartbreak is not weakness but testimony. It gives worth to silence, to the glances never returned, to the letters never read, to the tears wiped in moonlight. It gives a purpose to the stars we keep chasing inside ourselves.

In a world that rewards indifference, Celestial Romanticism chooses devotion.

It isn't just about writing poetry—it's about living it. When you look at the sky and feel your chest tighten with a name you can't forget, that's Celestial Romanticism. When your pulse echoes like a sonnet, when your hands tremble over the memory of their laughter, when every full moon reminds you of someone's absence—that's Celestial Romanticism. It turns those fragile emotions into altars.

And in those altars, we burn with love.

It allows the lover to remain a mystery, and the pain to remain poetic. Not every story needs a happy ending; some just need to be remembered in the rhythm of a verse. The poet in this realm does not seek applause—they seek connection, even if it's with a ghost, a whisper, or a feeling that no longer has a name.

Celestial Romanticism matters because it saves us. It preserves what is endangered: emotion, softness, sincerity. In its light, we remember how to believe in soulmates, stardust, and the sacred femininity of pain. It honours every feminine sigh, every aching boy who writes instead of speaks, every person who still cries when love leaves.

It tells you that even when they leave, you can stay. In the verse. In the metaphor. In the night sky.

Because love, in this genre, doesn't die—it transcends.

And that's why it matters.
Because it's not about being understood.
It's about being felt.

Even if that feeling breaks you, it will also write you into eternity.

- Amish Puri
Founder of Celestial Romanticism

How to write in Celestial Romanticism?

"Writing in Celestial Romanticism is a spectrum, in an attempt to find love, you get lost in love."

To write in Celestial Romanticism is to let your heart bleed stardust. It is to surrender your logic to longing, your ego to eternity, and your tragedies to tapestries of love. It is not a technique- it is a temperament. Let your emotional and vulnerable side flow as your tears, blood and sweat flow- like ink from whispered wounds, like one gaze at the moon and another at your muse. A touch remermbered can rewrite the stars from eternity. Pen down the metaphors of the cosmos with the smile of your muse.

Use poetic language but never loose vulnerable, emotional and a raw side of you, that you just can't forget, because beauty matters, but truth matters more- especially when it changes clothes in a strangers mirror with a bruised body through which blood seeps slowly drop by drop until it makes you feel that you didn't just fall for them- you orbitted them, as if a wish from the shooting star.

Celestial Romanticism is not written to impress, it is written to remember, to ache, and to eternalize what the world tries to forget.

Because love when written amongst the stars, it never dies.

In Celestial Romanticism, writing is more than just putting words together; it is a cosmic dance of the heart and mind. Crafting poetry inspired by the stars involves channeling the ethereal beauty of the universe into language. This post delves into how to approach writing within this genre, focusing on using celestial imagery to convey emotions that transcend the earthly experience.

Begin by invoking the vastness of space and the mystery of the cosmos. Consider how the stars and planets move in perfect harmony, much like love, constantly shifting yet unchanging in their essence. Use metaphors that align the human experience with the infinite—where hearts are galaxies, and love is the energy that holds everything together.

To capture the true spirit of celestial romanticism, focus on the light and darkness inherent in the universe. The juxtaposition of shadow and shine reflects the complexities of love—its joys and sorrows, its highs and lows. The moon, stars, and galaxies serve as a reminder that even in the darkest times, there is always light, always hope.

Experiment with poetic structures that echo the rhythm of the universe. You could use a repetitive, flowing cadence to symbolize the cycles of the moon or the endless journey of a comet. Rhyming couplets or free verse could mirror the constancy and unpredictability of celestial bodies.

Ultimately, celestial romanticism calls for a balance between the mystical and the emotional. By writing with an awareness of the universe's vastness, you connect the personal to the cosmic, giving your poetry a timeless quality.

-Amish Puri
Founder of Celestial Romanticism

Love

Love is that crimson-hued blood smeared across the **moon**
A wound that the universe stitched with a **silver spoon**,
Sacred like vermillion, embedded in starstruck souls,
To love, is to witness the **forever** eternal roles.

For those who seek an **end to love**, dancing in the shadow
Or those who preach the **paths of love**, weaving in the hollow,
Remember the burning **taste of love**, aching in the heart
Ever since one tastes a **sip of love**, to quench the thirst of every part,
Velvet ribbon wrapped elegantly across the stardust silk,
Engaged like a **bruised beauty**, pure and serene as milk,
Ringing in hearts like a bower **full of happiness**.

Yearning forever like a symphony of the **sun** and the **ocean**,
Aching beauty, with a **mellifluous melody** of the sun's devotion
Singing songs as it sets into the ocean's **unconditional love**
How ethereal it feels, as if an angel sent from the heaven's above,

As long as the sun creeps into the shadows of the earth
Doesn't matter how cruel the world has been in its inhuman dearth
It always shines in the earth's heart, no matter what, its **forever**

bright

To last in the **dreams of eternity**, like the dawn **sparkling light**

I feel that this is the true **essence of love's** deepest insight...

Longing

"What is longing?"

Longing is that old long-lost friend, you'd want to meet just one
more time
And hug her so tight, that even the stars will start to cry
Sleeping in the laps of the crescent moon's sad smile
To love like the love that we have always yearned for.

There will be days you don't get to see them quite often, but you
know what?
On the darkest days, I see that face, glistening bright with
melancholy
Getting to know her, makes me feel I just don't know her enough,
maybe I never will
Even then my love for her exists, in every tear, in every smile,
That I didn't even get to live as yet, that I didn't even get to cry as
yet
How cruel this world can be, that it does't even let me mourn this
loss of longing
Especially when I need a shoulder to weep, they give me a tissue to
wipe these oceans
Resting in the blanket of pain, maybe it's what feels more
comfortable now.

Gold like rose petals, is now full of thorns, trapped in this evil disdain of life,
Old and young leaves sprouting out of the earth, just to be stepped upon by miserable feet
Love when left too behind, becomes longing, as its always there but nowhere to be found
Dying feels easier at some point but longing keeps you hooked till an end which is never gonna come
Even when nothing lasts forever love and longing won't ever leave you
No matter where you go, as you sow, you shall you reap.

Through those cosmic pathways, people try to retrieve the love they never received,
Rhyming in vintage verses, a sequel of this bruised beauty that love owns,
In this celestial vault, love thrives for an eternity, and longing strives even after that
On the brightest days, it leaves you in an awestruck cycle of ethereal dreams.

Heartbreak

"What is Heartbreak?"

Heartbreak- The gut wrenching, soul ripping love which shatters
souls apart
As if a broken mirror bruises bloodshed wars within the brain and
the heart
Roaming around in the prison, where mirror lies on the slippery
floor
During the dusk, which sweeps away the stardust into the
oblivion's door.

Time and tide wait for none, for tide breaks the heart and time
heals it in forever,
Open ended at both sides, it strikes the surface at the ocean's shore
always and never.

Love letters you never get to send, just posting in your heart's mail
Over all these years striving in the silence of this storm kissed like
hail
Vibrant hues of love now whispers into the blackened cloud
Ever since that heart broke, even silence forgot how to be loud.

For I am the fractured fragment aching in the silence of every
scream,
Over and over again, love turns into lullabies I whisper in my

dream

Remnants of us still haunt the air-like promises inked and carved
on my skin,
Even time tests fate under the weight of what all could've been
Veins running without blood, where ink flows in them and blood
shows in paper
Every verse leaves a moist imprint on your heart- a melancholic
and silent shaper
Reincarnated in poetry, heartbreak is sorrow's silent draper.

Reunion

"What is Reunion?"

Reunion is the revival of the dead old past stars woven into
constellations
Especially an unfulfilled wish which comes true with the shooting
star
Under the heavenly scribes of the dreamy cosmic atmosphere
Never trying to find that bond, but to forever loose yourself in
that dream
I shall be unfettered under the spell of my foolish dreams I desire
Over the past few verses, I told a tale of love's unrelinquished fire
Nebulla dreams, woven into the tapestry of this sky's warm quest.

Yearning for love, makes it special, but you know what else does?
Attracting love by not longing for it anymore you see
Still Love, Longing, Heartbreak and Reunion go hand in hand
How Love craves longing, until it breaks into heartbreak, and still
chooses reunion.

And those who seek and end to love, love never ends
My dear if it ends, it was never love you see.
In this cosmic crime, only the guilty ones, who dare to love, fall
for this trap
Sweet, how love trap never ends, and just keeps your soul tied to

immortality,
How something called love, teaches us so well, what to stay alive
for.

Home to all, house to none, this is exactly what love means in
itself
Immortal being from the cosmic ocean of fire and earth, in the air
My dearest readers, do you think love can actually be defined?
And do you think it is fleeting moment or a lasting imprint?
No matteer how hard it is, why do you think people still love?
So many writers and poets died defining love, do you have a
definition for love?
How can you live and have no love story to tell?
Under this cosmic realm, come let's together explore this love...

1. Love

I saw her today.

Sitting on the bench with her textbook open, hair messed up and smile-the prettiest as usual. It was the first day of our class 11th. Everything was new those hallways, classrooms, teachers, subjects but one thing remained unchanged-my love for her.

"Yaden, come on bro! The new teachers have already entered the classroom." said Hadric

"Good morning class! My name is Ms. Ava, I'll be the class teacher of the non medical section, and Ms. Jessica will be the incharge of the medical ones. Let's begin with your introductions, shall we?"

Everyone started ranting about their names, hobbies as if someone gives a damn about them. My eyes remained locked with her honey coloured hair matching with her eyes. I believe she still loves me, her eyes says them all. The eyes chico, they never lie...

Suddenly Ms. Jessica our class teacher, and also our english teacher said to me,"Stand up, young man, tell us something about yourself."

"I...umm...am Yaden, Yaden Kyler-from Blacktown, Western Sydney. I am just an introvert and aspire to become a successful person in life."

"Mhm...I see, Well why is that handsome face veiled by this mask?" Ms. Jessica asked mockingly.

It was something so personal, Its been an year since covid ended and we were supposed to wear masks but now it became a part of my personality, a personality I started to develop after loosing all the confidence.

"Hello...Where are you lost sir?"

"Nothing, it just.. feels like me."

I brushed it off and the teacher continued with the introduction.

"Tell me something about yourself, beautiful butterfly!"

"My name is Ayla Junere, I recently came here from Auckland, New Zealand. Apparently, we shifted here two weeks ago. I love reading romance books, writing poems, dancing and listening to my favourite playlists."

Playlists? This word opened a world full of missing memories. The day she shared her playlist saying how dear it is to her. She smiled like a child, pure and wide. I still remember every song she ever shared, oh how I imagined us in every word, every lyric.

"Wonderful my dear, you may sit now."

Lectures began and teachers explained the curriculum to us. A typical first day at school. Not much workload, everyone were talking amongst themselves while I felt my eyes talking to her soul.

I saw her sitting with Sienna, talking amongst themselves.

Ayla turned back to talk with this guy sitting behind her, he seemed fat and amiable, quietly sitting over there, lost in his own thoughts. And suddenly she says to him,"Hi there, how's it going?"

"Brilliant!"

He said.

"We saw you were sitting alone lost somwhere, Sienna and I saw how you're writing something in that diary!"

"Oh! You mean this?" (points towards his journal)

"Well, I write...all the time, just penning down some thoughts of mine, how school can be overwhelming sometimes, how emotional I feel sometimes about it."

"Ah I see, well Ayla and I love to read, would you mind sharing with us those thoughts."

"Sure thing, Let's go!"

"Oh my god, that's actually really wonderful! Every word is a chef's kiss for real."

"It definitely is, good job!"

"Thank you so much! It really means a lot to me"

It seemed as if I don't care about who she talks to anymore, for me she's always been the one. I would fall on my knees and worship the ground she walks on, I ask god for her in my prayers. She breathes the air with passion, walks on my heart barefeet, all the time.

Day one of school came to an end so soon, all day I spent admiring my love.

Next day, Ms. Jessica decided to make the seating

arrangements. She asked that guy, the one with whom Ayla was talking, to sit behind me.

"My dear, you should engage yourself with someone, do one thing, you get up and sit behind Yaden."

He sat on the bench behind me and Hadric. So I decided to start a conversation. I don't know why.

"Hi bro, What's your name?"

"Asher, and you're Yaden, right?"

"Yes sir!"

"May I ask you something, if you don't mind?"

"Sure why not, go ahead."

"Yesterday you talked about your mask and it seemed you didn't quite well reciprocated about that, I felt that question made you feel a bit out of place, or am I just overthinking."

Oh, well till some extent he was right, I've been wearing that mask since so long and I don't know but sometimes I do feel a little insecure about my face. Sometimes it's just lack of confidence, mostly it's me.

"Actually, nothing much, as I said I am an introvert and couldn't exactly speak about my feelings at that time in front of all these new faces, but yeah thanks for checking in."

"Ah I see, well if you feel so, you can always share your thoughts."

"Thanks, I will"

I went out of the class in the lunch break with my best friend, Hadric, We've been together since class 10th and he seems to just...undertsand me and makes this life a little less miserable.

I came back inside the class to see that Ayla and Sienna were talking with Asher about songs and music.

"What's your favourite genre in songs?"

"Romance and songs about love, with soothing yet dazzling beats."

"I see, well I love that genre as well, I also seek solace in a little melancholic songs."

"Melancholic? But why? Who hurt you bro?"

"Not even a single scar came from my enemy, Sienna."

"I'm so sorry you've been through this, well was it friends or family?"

"Both"

They were talking and I realised that life is far away from fair. Someone is fighting their demons and still smiling. Even I do, my feelings aren't hidden by my smile but under this mask I wear. Do we stick to being sad because we can't move on or because those memories are too good to be forgotten?

"We seek comfort in things which hurt us and maybe that's why we choose to bleed on the paper." said Asher while reading out his work to Ayla and Sienna.

Did this guy, just read my mind, or...nevermind. If god want us to be together, we shall forever remain in the embrace of each other, till then I am waiting for her after all this time. Always...

I sat down on my seat and Asher saw me, and sat beside me as I asked him to. We started to talk and I realised that he does understand me, without me having to say anything as if we know each other since forever.

"You know the other day we went into the library me, Ayla and Sienna had so much fun, we got three books and..."
I don't know what he was saying after that but he seemed passionate about it, I was already following him on his social media through mutuals but for the first time we talked. I went home and saw him sending me videos on instagram, random talks and all. I added him to our boys groupchat, it was me, Hadric, Kevin, and now Asher. I sent a random video about a cute people to which he said,"Oh so you've got a girlfriend, huh?"
"Ex"
"Ah I see, who's her?"
"Ayla"
"Oh my god, so like do you still like her?"
"*Love"
"Oh, well I didn't know anything about it, so tell me more about it."
"Absolutely sir!"

I felt this guy seems trustworthy, I told him. Everything.

"September 16th. The day our relationship began, two days

before my birthday. She liked and replied to my instagram stories, we talked and I told her how much I adored her and she said she felt the same and we finally started dating each other. It was really dreamy like fairytale, you know, I fell first and she felt harder."

"Oh my god, so like, straight out of a romance book?"

"Much likely"

"But like, why did you guys breakup then?"

"We never ended on good terms, you know? We fought several times, there were tons of misunderstandings and miserable people with no sense of self, with hearts full of jealousy who put their evil eye on our relationship."

"But it should be you guys against the world, not you people against each other, oh my god!"

"No, Asher it is not as simple as it seems, it was... very complicated and people made it worse."

"So like, can't we do something about it now?"

"I don't know, I have tried for atleast a million times, I will still try and wait for her, till the day she comes to me and we will be back together."

"So when did you guys breakup?"

"After dating for some six months, on the day of our class 10th farewell, she returned me all the things I gave her, the daisy pendent, my belongings, most importantly my love for her, while her hairtye and the ring she gave me I still cherish them as a memory form her. One day during class 10th, we even got into trouble because of this, our class teacher got to know about this and even our parents were called."

"So like what happened after that?"

"Nothing much, we got away with it, after that we both cried on the farewell day, Sienna was looking after Ayla and I shared my heart with Hadric, we were just crying and I don't know but even now I'm telling this to you I feel I am reliving those moments again. Wounds still freshly cut, with blood dripping out of my throat."

"I'm so sorry that you went through all that, but you know what? I really want to help you to get back with her, no matter what,"

"Wait, really? But how do you plan to do it?"

"I will require your support and trust."

"I am with you always and I trust you'll do your best."

"Okay, so tell me, how do I talk to her, because I don't think talking to her in school will help us, we barely have 15 minutes in the lunch break."

"So listen, I'll give you her social media account, send her the request and she'll accept it, for sure."

"Done sir."

He sent her the request, in the mean time I told him about our relationship in detail, how far we went for love, about every song she shared telling me how much she loved me, our matching profile pictures, school romantic moments, holding hands, how I made a list of all the korean dramas she loved watching, in short everything.

A few hours later Asher texted me,"Hey bro, she accepted the request."

"Excellent!"

"Now text her, and send her this video."

It was the video of a song she loved a lot. I wanted to remind her of each and every moment we spent together, every lyric, every word. And what happened next, blew my mind.

"Bro, she didn't respond quite well with the song." said Asher.

"Oh she must have forgotten, no worries."

Forgotten? That was not even the question in the first place, of course she didn't forget about those words which made me fall in love with her. First love can't be forgotten. Neither can I.

"So now how do I get to initiate the conversation about you both?"

"Just talk to her and mention me casually, we'll see where it goes."

"Yes sir."

It was that day when I told significant things to Asher regarding all the people who tried to create misunderstandings between us, she got frustrated from the toxic enviornment and the already existing misunderstanding grew into our separation.

"Bro send her this song, she can't deny not knowing this song."

"As you say sir."

This time I wasn't dissapointed, she responded with a pleasant tone, explaining how much connected she feels to the song. Music it is, which can't let the fire of love, fade away. It is what connects you to the soul.

"Yay! Bro she responded so happily like a child, wow we got it right this time."

"Wohoo! Exactly, we did it, now tell her randomly that Yaden sent you this song."

"Done!"

"What she said?"

"She said, 'Oh well I see, I do admire this song a lot."

Does she admire the song? Or our memories hidden in those lyrics? Or does she have someone else in her life? So many questions poppping up inside my head. Ayla and Asher almost became good friends, maybe it will help Asher to open up to her about me. This continued several times exchanging songs, thoughts, videos, but now it was time for exchanging a korean drama reference.

"Bro you should try this korean drama, it's so much fun, you'll definitely not regret it." said Ayla

"For sure, I will." Asher replied.

Well, it was the same drama she asked me to watch, and told me how much he loved it, she said it reminded her about me. And now it's what reminds me of her. I told Asher about this, he was struck in his emotions and became more determined, he said,"We all love a soul ripping, jaw dropping romance story. It seems like a fictional trope, coming to life." Attempts after attempts, and then it happened.

"So by the way, Asher, do you know he's my ex?"

She herself asked this to him.

"Umm... yes I do."

"Yeah"

"So like how did you guys breakup, if you're comfortable sharing?"

"Why? Your 'friend' didn't tell you, huh?"

"Oh, well...umm"

"Haha, just kidding. Alright let me tell you."

"Oh, I got scared, anyways, go on"

"Yeah, basically our relationship got very toxic, I gave him so many chances, but there were many trust issue based incidents where he couldn't justify his actions."

Really? Well I know I did make a few mistakes, at that time I wasn't much mature about certain situations where I couldn't handle some things, people literally interferred to the point where our relationship couldn't survive at that time. That doesn't mean we were the only ones at fault. Now I know how to handle tough situations. And people who made it worse.

"Why don't you give him another chance, Ayla?"

"Asher, you don't know I've given him many chances but all he did was loose all of them."

"For once, take decision from your heart and not just brain, I understand he did mistakes, and no matter what I say, those mistakes can't be retrieved, but have you ever seen an elderly couple? For how many times did they forgive each other to end up here."

"You're right Asher, I understand you're rying to help your friend, but why do I have to give a reason for my happiness? Why always me?"

"Mhm...I see, well maybe it is because you guys never had a closure, it just ended on bad terms without a proper conclusion. Take your time, no issues and think about it."

By this time, our summer vacations just began and I asked Asher, not to touch this matter so that things can slow down a bit, without rushing too much. A few weeks passed, I shared my thoughts, emotions and feelings with Asher, he understood them quite well, without me having to say it. We started to develop a great bond. By this time, he became my best friend. Hadric and Asher knew each other as they studied in class 7 together, the year when Asher was new to this school. We three formed the best unstoppable trio, our friendship felt iconic. Almost a month later, we returned back to school as they reopened. Now Ayla and Asher talked about this matter of our relationship during free time like lunch breaks, free periods and even through social media. As our holidays got over, we gave our exams which were right after.

Almost three months since this session started, and still Ayla wasn't convinced to talk to me. But what didn't stop me, was this friendship we shared, no matter how hard it was, we always found a way.

After all this time, Ayla got to know my perspective better through Asher and I got to know hers from him, at this point of time, Asher was trying his best and said,"I know it's hard, but just because it's taking time, doesn't mean it's not happening, I wanna give you this gift of retrieving your relationship with Ayla on your birthday, by September." I believe this is something which kept me going.

Our term exams noticed dropped by mid july, they will start in August and end in September, we were in full preperation mode and also under the tension of the workload we had, but at the end we got away with it.

In between the exams Asher's birthday came on September 8, it was a day to remember. I texted him at midnight to make him feel special, he was the happiest and glad like a child.

Very few people came to school that day, our biology teacher Ms. Diva, with whom we were the most comfortable with, when I told her about Asher's birthday she started singing it out loud in the whole class all joined. Asher said,"Thank you so much bro, it was literally the best birthday ever." He's done so much for me and simply gets me.

Exactly one day before my birthday, that is on 17th September, Asher gave me the best news ever, Ayla agreed to talk to me, although as friends but it was enough for now for us to sort things out. He made this groupchat where it was just us three.

"Hi guys! Great to see you both together after an eternity."

"I don't know what to say."

"Asher, you remember what I told you? Just friends."

"Yes, exactly."

"Yes ma'am, he told me everything."

"Good."

"Mhm"

"Alright guys, you guys are talking after so long, I'd give you guys some space...Also Yaden don't forget to update me later! Gotta go, All the best!"

Asher left and we both shifted to personal messages, I did initiate the conversation. It felt very overwhelming and emotional after talking to her. I didn't know what to say, talking to her again made me feel alive.

"So, how are you?"

"Good, what about you?"

"Was just thinking about you."

"So, you didn't move on?"

"You know."

"So you didn't, huh?"

"Mhm..."

"Yaden, listen, I respect your feelings and love for me but I am telling you I have moved on and I don't want to be in a relationship, being with me will just hurt you more, I want you to be happy, even if I am not there."

"Ayla you know I can't be happy without you."

"I really want to have time, I really enjoy your company as a friend but right now I don't wanna be in any relationship, because last time it ruined my ability to process my emotions, with my vulnerable side and you know how much I hate that side of mine."

"No worries, take your time, and I am waiting for you, like

always."

Later that night we talked about us a lot. I will wait for her, till the time vanishes and fades away my soul into oblivion. For her, a million times over.

"Bro, how did it go?"

"Thank you so much bro, you literally gave me the best gift ever, talking to her again feels like a dream come true, though she clearly said she need more time and wants to be friends for now, But I will try my best to get her back, to get my Ayla back."

"Oh my god bro, I'm geniunely so happy for you, like it's amazing, also don't worry I am with you and I will help you whenever you need me."

"You know I'm feeling so overwhelmed right now, I don't know what to say, you did so much for me, I don't think so that I'll be able to pay you back."

"Oh god, shut up bro, you don't need to pay me back, it's my greatest pleasure to see you happy again, now you better get rid of that mask."

"Promise, done, thank you so much once again!"

It was midnight, I got a happy birthday text from my bestfriends, Hadric and Asher. Asher wrote a big poem for me, while Hadric wrote a heartful message, and you know the best part was the, 'Happy Birthday Yaden!' text from Ayla. I felt so happy that I got no words to describe it.

"It was a great one, Ayla even texted me Happy Birthday!"

"Yes! exactly, I told you she won't deny being with you."

"Yeah, but we're just friends for now as she said."

"Just friends? Do you not know that how she sometimes look at you in class, with the soul devouring, heart ripping gaze? 'Just friends' do not look at each other in that way."

"Wait, really?"

"No, just kidding"

"Damn it, Asher, stop feeding my delusions with your poetic soul"

"Haha lol"

"Wait, I've got an idea from these stupid delusions."

"Really? What?"

"You write poems right?"

"Ah yes, so now you're saying we should write poems on your past love life to make her fall for you again?"

"Yes, my boy, exactly!"

"Oh my god, well that's a pretty good idea you fetched from my poetic yapping."

"I love your yapping"

"Oh my god bro, stop!"

"Okay, so let's get to the point I'll tell you an incident and you write poems about it and send her one by one when I tell you too, so it doesn't feel heavy on her."

"Got it sir."

I told him about the golden dot theory, we made out of love, one day she asked me, what will you do if I got lost in a crowd to which I replied,"You are my golden dot that I will identify in the crowdiest area and in the darkest place, you are my happiness that can be found in the darkest of the times, because you are my light, that I'll forever remember to turn on." This was one of the many incidents I told Asher to which he dedicately wrote poems for, and sent it one by one every week, it did make an impact and it changed the way she used to talk to me, some memories bring back the soft side of ours we lost.

Asher and Ayla are both writers, they even gave poems in the school magazine, both of their poems got selected, somewhere in July and now it was nearly november and he came with the school poetry book.

"Look guys, Ayla and my poems have been published in the school poetry book, I'm so happy wow."

"Wow bro, we did it."

"We definitely did."

"Congratulations Asher and Ayla, I'm so proud you both."

"Yay! Thank you so much bro!"

"Thanks." she said

We slowly start to talk much more than ever, at this point of time, Ayla, Sienna, Hadric, Asher and I became the most iconic friend group. We were the most happening group of our class. We also made a writing account started by Asher to post his poems. When I told him that we used to have onc earlier but we deleted it, after Ayla and I... parted ways. Hearing this, Asher said,"It's not just my account, it's ours, we'll post together." Later Ayla joined and started to post as well, I was so happy as now I could reciprocate my feelings for her in those editing styles, music, pictures, and of course the poems based on our situations which Asher wrote.

December knocked at our door, making me feel all those memories we once cherished. The winter arc you know, I think it opens the pathways of all the best memories and the worst pains. Asher ranted to me about his past problems, his ever lasting generational trauma and family issues, how we got tortured in his past tuition, went through many friendship breakups and a lot more. I talked with him about all the people who tried to break us apart.

"Karma is always watching, Yaden, don't you worry, we've got this. Always remember, we are divinely protected, anyone who did us wrong, would end up in a situation, much worse."

I believed it and kept patience. In mid December, our school took us on a trip to an educational research centre. We quite well enjoyed it, and clicked pictures after the event. For the first time in two years, we posted a picture, though it was the five of us, but still, it was a picture with me and her in it. I adored her smile everytime I looked at that picure. It was going perfect, but destiny had his own plans.

Kevin from that group chat who was a friend to us, posted a picture of me, Hadric and Asher making fun of us three and writing random rumours to put down our friendship. I showed it to Asher and Hadric, at first they were angry, which later faded away, but I blocked him. Hadric seemed to brush it off, Asher said,"Those who couldn't match your level, try to raise their own, by putting others down, let them cry about it, our friendship is stronger than their insecurities."

He said what he said. A few days later, I started to talk to Ayla more about us, and tried to convince her so that we can get back into a relationship, that too in the group chat only. A few days passed and new year was approaching as we stepped into the last week of december.

On December 30th, we were talking amongst ourselves, in the group and I said something which upsetted her. I sent her a video about relationships and how we should put our decisions first and treat our friends opinions as opinions and not the final decisions of our lives. It aggitated her, and she stopped typing in the group and started texting me personally.

"Yaden, I've told you so many times, we can't be more than friends. How many times do I have to tell you it was my own decision, not my friend's decision, she did give me her opinion but the final decision was mine."

She got upset and angry and she started to breakout, things got serious and it happened. Exactly what I feared the most.

She blocked me.

Again.

I sent screenshots of our chats to Asher and explained him everything.

"No, no, no. Oh my god, I'm so sorry bro, let's fix this, this can't be real..."

"Asher, let it happen."

"But bro-"

"I said let it happen. It's okay, I'll just need sometime."

"Okay bro listen, I understand, don't worry, everything will be just fine and I am always there for you, no matter what, share with me everything that's going in your heart, anytime. I'm just one call away!"

New year dawned upon us, I pretended as if everything was okay. I tried to distract myself. New year wishes were shared amongst us friends. I almost lost hope because I know the real reason, she denied our relationship was...something else. And I haven't yet told Asher about it.

"Asher, I need to tell you something very important!"

"Yes sir, all ears!"

2. Longing

I'm dying.

Oh my god, not again. I don't know what's happening to me again. Is he really back? Or am I just daydreaming. He has to understand I don't want to break his heart later, we belong to different castes, my parents would never, in a million years, agree to this marriage. The last I would do is to break his heart. I do not want that in any case. This society is built that way, and I don't know what to do.

Our final practical exams have basically started and I'll to secure good grades, else my parents wil kill me. I don't want to disappoint them. I've got to study and I want him to focus on studies too. Meanwhile, Hadric's birthday came on February 1st, the trio shined like always where Yaden and Asher wished and celebrated Hadric's birthday. Followed by our class 11th farewell, they clicked pictures. Yaden and I were a part of the singing choir, that day we were supposed to wear a black shirt, I didn't had one and buying a shirt for one day, felt like a wastage to me. I asked Yaden to bring an extra shirt for me. I wore his shirt that day, it was the best farewell ever.

At this point, I was spending my time mostly studying and the exams were approaching, every day feels more scary as the exam date approached. We all gave our exams, which honestly went pretty average, much less than our expectations. Asher and I, didn't stop discussing about that matter, he constantly told me, how Yaden was sad and isolated all day. Exams were going on and in between the preparatory holidays, Asher texted me, trying to convince me to talk to him. I lost it.

"Ayla, please listen, atleast talk to him, I promise we won't ask you for anything more than being just friends."

"Try to understand my point of view bro, we can't be just friends...He might fall for me again and I can not keep on breaking his heart again and again."

"Ayla, take decision on your own, don't let someone tell you to leave your boyfriend just because they hate him."

"Asher, for how many times I need to tell you that it was my independent decision and just a suggestion from my bestfriend, Tyla. I can't with this. For how many do I have to give a reason for my happiness?"

I started crying, Asher did apologise, but when it comes to protecting my own peace, I don't care who he or she is, I'll simply cut the off, and that's exactly what I did here. I stopped replying to his texts either. He must have told this to Yaden, as usually he tells everything to him. I don't know what happened after that but all of a sudden I started to feel bad about it, I understand he's just trying to help his best friend and I respect that but that doesn't mean that you can play with my mental peace. Anyways, after a few days when Asher saw me in school during our next exam, he was about to wave a hi to me, it was exactly what I was about to do, but then we both remembered at the same time, that we had a fight, after coming home I checked the common writing account we made, but I saw it was logged out, I thought Asher changed the password because we had a fight, and I unblocked Yaden to ask him about this.

"Has Asher changed the passoword of the writing account?"

He was definitely shocked to see my unexpected message but he said.

"Umm... let me ask him real quick."

He replies after a while," Ayla I did ask him but he said he never did anything like that so it must be a technical glitch or something."

Asher was stunned as well when he saw me texting Yaden out of nowhere, he constantly texted Yaden to know more about it, but Yaden was talking to me as I came out randomly with this surprise, but things weren't as good as we thought.

"Bro, tell me everything, what she said, also I didn't change any passwords?"

"Okay, wait, don't go anywhere."

He waited for a few minutes and when Yaden didn't reply to him as he was talking with me, Asher texted me.

"Hey, Ayla, I never changed the passwords, okay?"

"Bro, you literally texted me after a full week just to say that."

"I know I'm really sorry, that day also I wanted to bid you a lii, but then..."

"Mhm, I understand, I didn't like this either, can we be friends again?"

"Sure, why not!"

This sorting out between us seemed sweet but who knew it would change our entire lives.

"Yaden, bro, Ayla and I sorted it out, we're friends again!"

"You must be very happy, right?"

"Why, are you not happy we got back together?"

"Bro why didn't you listen to me when I asked you not to text her?"

"Umm...I though you were busy talking to her, I didn't want to bother you...But I don't understand why are you so mad at me?"

"What's the benefit when you can't even listen to what I say? Why are you so impatient? Couldn't you just wait for a second? You know what go to hell, I'm not talking to you anymore, bye!"

Asher kept begging for months for Yaden to stop, he barely had any friends and he didn't wanna loose Yaden now, but now he did, although Asher didn't do anything wrong, but he couldn't control his emotions sometimes. Yaden told me several times how he's clingy and invades his personal space sometimes, unknowingly. This friendship breakup along with mine and Yaden's separation, shattered our friendgroup into fragments, which seemed almost impossible to join. For many months Asher couldn't move on, Hadric was his only best friend at that time and as the new sessions started, class 12th, Hadric and Asher went to the same tuitions, Hadric tried his best to fix Asher, and when Yaden and Asher stopped talking completely, Yaden who never gave a damn about it, Asher was also on the same page now. Months later of this tragedy, Asher, Yaden and I started to focus on ourselves, our grades, body, and mental health.

I still can't believe, a friendgroup which felt like family, got burnt alive. Asher even stopped talking to me for a few weeks, but seeing him alone and isolated all day in class, many classmates, teachers were concerned about him, he who yapped and laughed all day, was a non chalant mess full of depressing thoughts. He dropped many pounds, became more serious about his writing and started to work on writing his first book, earlier he wrote a book for Yaden, which he released on Hadric's birthday, as a gift for Hadric as it was his birthday and Yaden, as the book was a fanfiction about Harry Potter. Yaden was a potterhead and he made Asher watch Harry Potter for the first time. Meanwhile, Yaden seemed to develop a good physique, better grades and overall execution at school, even I started to perform the best in biology, it was by far my favourite subject. It cut my long brown hair short, as a symbolism to give up on this miserable past, long ago. On the other hand, Asher and Yaden grew their hair longer. Girls cut their hair short to let go of the memories, and boys grow them to embrace them, I feel no one talks about it much.

"Hi bro, Are you okay ?"

"Mhm, just a bit of overthinking, nothing else. What about you?"

"Same. Listen don't be upset about Yaden."

"I don't wanna talk about someone whom I helped and I got

this in return. We even had a fight because of him. Hadric is the only companion right now, even he says that I am not at fault."

"I understand Asher, but all we must do is move on from them and work on ourselves."

It's easy to say move on, but only the one who goes through this much trauma, knows how hard it is for them. "It's now time to make people regret and reconsider their choices. Let us don't chase, but attract them." He said.

I wanted to leave my past self and explore more, I don't deserve this vulnerability. Let me treat myself like who I am. I started to talk with this guy named Alex. He was an average looking guy, but very nice and sweet to me. Whenever I needed anything, he was the first one to help, I felt really impressed and after a month of talking stage, he told me how he had a crush on me for the past few weeks and oh my god, I never expected it from him. Alex was a quiet kid sitting in a corner of the class, a much introverted guy who was a bit...nerdy. I obviously wasn't ready for a relationship at this point and I denied, we talked a lot though as friends but I didn't let the proposal affect our bond.

I thought, maybe one day I'll get the real love of my life. I told Asher about it and he was struck in shock,"Oh my god, Alex? Really, are you kidding me, he didn't."

"Yes, he did."

"Gosh Ayla, Yaden will be disappointed for real."

"Will he?"

We both laughed it off, though it was serious because the way Alex said," You taught me the meaning of love, I never believed in love until I saw you." It sounded so real, although I guess I'll have to distance myself from Alex, otherwise he might get more attached which will hurt him later. For now my main focus is our term examinations. I so want to score the best in these. Asher told he's working on his book, Yaden... he seemed to have worked a lot on himself, whether it's controlling his anger, irritation on minor inconvenience and he skills. I got know from Asher that Yaden has started to work as a freelancer by editing videos and started to make money. He got to know this from Hadric. Though the tension resides, but the way Hadric helped Yaden in school and Asher in tuitions, by being with them to help them get over through these traumatic incidents, was truly remarkable. He was a true friend to both of them. Sienna and I constantly supported Asher with his first book. He was also supported my his reader friend, Diana, at this point, Asher and Diana, worked together in class, whether it's about reading, writing or any discussions. He was mostly seen with her. I don't know but all my friends seem to find an escapism. I couldn't, Sienna and Asher were there for me platonically, but the ocean in me, craved for the sun.

"Bro, I finally published my first book ever, Oh my god!'

"Yay bro, you did it, honestly we all are so proud of you!"

"Finally, now I am a published author, Hadric, Sienna and Diana will be so happy, yay!"

"They definitely will, teachers, coordinators, principal and the whole school management will be amazed."

Writing a book at this age, was such a big thing. Earning money as a freelancer at this age, absolutely stunning. Maybe this separation was necessary, for the character development of both of these guys. Everything happens for a reason. Maybe Yaden and I parted ways because...of some reason.

There's this guy, who felt quite intimidating to me. Parker. The way he looked at me while I was sitting on my bench...that look was just soul ripping. He saw me looking back at him, and simply came walking towards me whispering something to his friend. I looked away and he sat on the bench in front of me. I felt his presence but ignored him, had my lunch, and walked out the classroom. As I came back, I saw him sitting next to my seat. I sat on my seat and he looked at me. He initiated the conversation.

"Ayla, right?"

"Mhm"

"Well, I saw you sitting alone today, what happened?"

"Umm, I...actually my friends didn't come today so..."

"Oh, well can I join you, if you don't mind?"

"Sure!"

We talked about ourselves a bit, he seemed quite invested in knowing my story. I felt I could trust him, and I did tell him about my past relationships, I never felt so comfortable with a guy in so long. I looked at him with a soft passion in my eyes. I could see the fire in his quick movements, and the burning desire of being in my presence.

Next day Sienna and I were having lunch, he came to us and started his flirty talks. Sienna noticed us, gave a smirk and left me alone with him. He started to talk about exam preperations,"How's biology preperation going on?"

"Well, I'm still on genetics, what about you?"

"Oh, I'm all done."

"Really? That's wonderful, how did you manage to do all that so soon?"

"Actually, I have notes that Ms. Diva gave us before leaving the school, you can give me your WhatsApp number, I'll send you those notes."

"Perfect, that's wonderful, note my number."

That day we exchanged numbers and from then onwards we started to talk. Notes weren't shared, pasts were. He shared his horrible past and I sympathised with him. Villains are not born, they are made. After one to two months of our talking stage, we started to date. For the first time ever, I felt safe in so long. Everyone in class started to notice us, and it was quite obvious. I never got this close to anyone ever. It was a dream. We got to know each other more through social media. One day I saw his instagram story. He was drinking in it. It changed my whole perspective of him, so I decided to confront him.

"What's about the instagram story, huh? You drink?"

"Ah, no Ayla actually it's not me, some of my friends do. It's just a story, you trust me right?"

"Mhm. Right, maybe I was overthinking."

Or maybe I was right! I couldn't believe my eyes, I hope it was just a story. He sounded like a song and moved like wind. He asked me if...we could be in a relationship, and I said yes. We were in a happy relationship for a few months, we used to take biology classes together. We even sat together in painting class and shared some special time together. I felt comfortable and I thought, now it's the right time to tell Asher and Sienna about this.

"Hi bro, I've got to tell you something interesting!"

"Wait what, what's it?"

"So Parker and I have started to date!"

"Oh my god, what on the earth, are you serious?"

"Yes bro, I know it's shocking but it is what it is."

"Gosh Ayla, well Sienna and I already got hints, you guys are always together, and we saw how you talk to him, and he talks to you."

"Umm...haha lol, nevermind."

"But bro, he's not a very good guy, but since you're in a relationship, I trust you must have seen some side of him, filled with love for you!"

"Yeah, exactly. Also just wanted to apologise for not keeping in touch."

"It's okay, I understand you must be super invested in your relationship with him. It's okay, take your time and if you feel the need to share anything we are always here."

I know Asher was disappointed, even if he didn't say it. Some similar reaction was shown by Sienna. And I think it is because Parker does not hold a very good reputation in school. He's been involved in many fights in school. Also, his friendship with some badass seniors and his company wasn't quite nice about him. But I feel it is because of his traumatic childhood. His emotinally unavailable father who used to beatm him, he lost his mother long ago. I felt at this point of time, I could fix him.

The school hallways,with just us and no one else, were filled with sunshine in the warm winter days. I remember us having deep emotional talks, we were talking and then an awkward silence between us started to take over. I felt something different in the air, a strong spicy scent fading into the corridors and then the moment came. The long, much awaited kiss between us finally happened.

I was born in the ocean, raised by the fire
Taught how to tremble, not to desire,
But something tonight-no wind, no flame
Left me untamed and whispered a name.
The moon bowed lower than she ever has been,
And a sigh broke loose where silence had been,
Not thunder, not storm, yet my breath did shake,
As if time itself forgot how to wake.
Not lost, not gone-just no longer the same,
Like the hush that follows when you whisper a name.
The ocean within me learned how to burn,

And the fire forgot it could never return.

"Ayla! Ayla, where are you? come on get up! "

"Uh, yes mom just coming."

Oh my god! I have no idea what to feel. I checked open his texts. For a few days everything went right. Not anymore though. I don't know why but the sweetest guy ever turned into such a monster, he talked to me very rudely and we started to have many fights. All the limits felt crossed when he started to verbally abuse me. I stopped talking to him in school and he seemed not to care, as if all he cared about was...me in a lustful manner. I asked god why can't I get someone who truly loves me and not just for my body. One morning I saw his instagram story, it was the same bottle of alcohol. I asked him," You lied to me, didn't you? You do drink and that day also..." He cut me off mid sentence and barked," Yes, I did lie to you. I drink and it's all your fault, You gave me stress, so much stress after those daily fights!"

I stopped talking. Only a weak and coward would do something like that. I mean what on the earth was that manipulation going on. He tried to put the blame of his stupidity on me. I told this whole matter to Asher to which he said," Only those who fail to express themselves intelligently, stick to abuse." As for Sienna, she was deeply hurt and sad for me. I did cry for a day or two but then I realised a guy who drinks alcohol on minor inconvenience, uses girls for his lust and abuses verbally, aren't worth crying for. Grudges? Maybe. Going back? Never.

Anyways, I started to completely focus on myself because we had our exams approaching and guess what. This time I performed better in most subjects, so did Asher, Sienna and rest of our friends. Everyone wanted to focus on final practicals and examinations for now. We did spend some extra time in school studying and getting our doubts cleared. All assignments and notes given to us by teachers truly helped us. At this point everyone's only priority was their studies.

"Asher, I've to tell you something, bro."

"Absolutely, go ahead."

"Well, Parker and I..."

"Broke up?"

"Wait, yes, but how did you know?"

"You guys went from sitting together to ignorning each other, how did I not know?"

"Mhm, Point."

"Yes"

"Now, how did it happen and why?"

"Actually, he got very abusive in small fights. He disrespected me and...he drinks."

"Wait, what the actuall hell? He drinks? Did you knowk about this before the breakup?"

"Maybe. Yes, I saw a bottle of alcohol, he posted its picture on his instagram story, and..."

"You got fooled?"

"Yes, he lied to me. He deceived me and manipulated me into thinking it's my fault and he started to drink because of our relationship issues. But he did this, from much before."

"Oh my god Ayla, breathe, so did you guys do anything private?"

"Like what?"

"Like a kiss?"

"Yes"

"On the lips or just a casual?"

"On the lips."

"Okay, leave. Well now you've got a lesson that you can't fix a broken glass, didn't you?"

"Mhm."

I don't know why, but this was hella embarrassing. I I expected that he will last forever unlike anyone else but he very well prooved me wrong. Anyways, I think I did all this because at this point I moved on from Yaden. He used to take such good care of mine. He never treated me like I'm not worth it or something. He literally worshipped the ground I walked on. But, do I wanted to go back to him? No, it was too late now. I know it was not late enough for him to accept us back but, for the society it was. What will the people around us say? Nevermind. I guess I couldn't trust these men now. All I want is to grow and glow up with my friends.Also, I need a break from all of these idiotic events happened recently. God forbid a girl finds her true love.

I got really inspired from Asher on publishing his first book. Since I am also a writer, I tried to write on too and guess what? I did it. It was a short poetic deliberation of my heart, unlike

Asher's deep and intense book about the seven phases of love in sufism, well structured with sections, with great poems in each section. Mine consisted of narrating a story of a girl in love, in the form of poetry. It was a rather short and cute one. I felt as if I wrote a part of my heart in the search of love. Maybe one day love will find me. The one with pure, romantic love which makes you feel alive.

It was just two months left for the most awaited farewell of our 12th grade. Our vice principal and Coordinator chose Asher and me to represent the Science stream while giving the speech on the farewell day in a dual perspective version. But Ms. Jessica, our english teacher wanted more students. She prepared us and selected a few students including me, Sienna, Asher, Diana and more. We were so excited for it and planned our speeches a month before. As we stepped into the new year of 2025, our farewell preperations like outfit checks, our speeches all set, the plannings, discussions, like everything possible was being done.

"Ayla, so this is the speech, add your part and let me know any refinements you feel."

"Done."

The speech was put forward through thourough deliberations and discussions until it was finally ready for us to perform. It was somwhere around 5 minutes including both of our parts. As per the requirements and guidelines of the speech, we made it. We religiously worked on it as we got to know that it will be a really proud moment for us. We practised the speech on voice messages and in class as well. Everything was going well. It was time for our final practical exams before the farewell procession. We were a little worried as we wanted to give our best. Though our preperations were on point, we still felt anxious as for the first time the practicals were not be conducted by our school teachers.

External examiners were supposed to come from different schools and take our practical and viva-voce based exams to give us marks as a part of the internal assessments. Everyone wanted to perform their best as this was a saviour for their percentage to reach to the next level. It could make or break the game.

I realised this and therefore worked hard, our exams went well. We literally stood there for good long six hours on the day of our painting practical, I still remember how hard it was. But atleast all our practicals went really well. It was like a big load off our chests.

Now we could focus on the farewell again. We were really excited but then, something happened which ruined our excitement.

3. Heartbreak

Ayla and Asher's speeches got cancelled at the last minute. I got to know this when I reached at the farewell venue. Hadric and Asher were talking about it. I overheard their conversation how hard they both were preparing for it but it got cancelled because of a limit for the number of speakers. They are the best writers and speakers I know. I don't understand why this happened at the last minute. Though Ms. Jessica was an amazing teacher but this act of hers, upsetted Ayla and Asher, obviously if someone was preparing for something with so much dedication, they will feel bad about it.

At this point I was overthinking as I felt my reaction towards Asher was real bad. I overreacted and now I wanted to apologise to him. He's been such a great friend to me, I did him wrong. I wanted to say sorry today on the farewell, but seeing his uncontrolable expressions, I knew it was not a good day for it. He might feel that why did I come to him after months of my actions. Anyways, I feel that every good moment was somewhere lost in the past. The farewell was lit, we did enjoy so much, danced, had good food, amazing speeches and performances. Both Asher and Ayla had their stage moments as they participated in a small contest. They carried themselves well. Later, we had the felicitaion ceremony where Asher and Diana won prizes. Hadric and I got our pictures clicked and later Asher and Hadric got their pictures done. But I felt our trio, or should I say the iconic trio as Asher said, couldn't get a trio picture. It was...sad. The day went well and very emotional. We got back home and I was thinking about Ayla. She looked so beautiful, I could admire her for a lifetime.

I started to think about the first time we ever talked. She followed me on instagram. We were in grade 10, and one day she replied to my story and we started to talk. It turned into a wholesome conversation as we started to get to know each other better everyday. Gradually, we started to develop an undying affection and liking for each other. We participated in many activites in our school together. One such event helped us to work on building this bond. I remember how in that school cultural event, we got a lot of time to talk, we used to walk in the corridors and exchanged words with each other. On a fine day, September 16, that is exactly two days before my birthday. We were texting each other how we like us better when we're together. We used to go in the school playground during lunch breaks, eating together, having our daily chit-chat sessions. We used to hold hands and talk. No lust, only love. It was so good going but then it happened. Our first fight.

I don't exactly remember what it was but we were mature enough to understand that all couples fight and we are just teenagers trying to love each other. We sorted it out and that night we spent time with each other online. Just us. No one else.

During our school assembly, she stood there in the ground just like all of our classmates. But she shined different. Wrapped in the warm embrace of the sunlight, she looked so gorgeous that I couldn't stop admiring her. She loked at me and I was already adoring the love of my life.

"What?"

"Nothing. Just adoring my baby."

"Aww, you're such a flirt."

"Only for you baby."

"Oh my god, I can't stop blushing."

"As you should, babygirl."

We came to school in the morning in separate buses but I used to wait for her, I went near her school bus and we went inside together. We love holding hands. One day I came to my class and she was walking on the staircase, nobody was their but us. I took a moment and held her hand. It was a soul ripping connection. She smiled so hard, and just couldn't stop blushing. She bragged about it to all her friends, how I held her hand. We talked about this as a metaphor for holding on to us and never taking a step back, no matter what.

I gifted her a ring on a random day in class. She was so happy to see it. It was the first gift I ever gave her. Seeing her reaction, I made gift giving as my love language. She said it reminds her of me. After a few days, this time I gave her an evil eye bracelet to forever protect our relationship.

"It's gonna last forever right?...You and I"

"Forever. Promise."

"Just us."

"Yes love, just us."

"Yay!"

Everything seemed perfect, we enjoyed ourselves and late night video calls became a part of our daily routine. We just to discuss about our zodiac signs. She was a Pisces and I was a Virgo. How these completely opposite zodiacs, complemented each other so well that it seemed as if god blessed us from the heavens above. During our video calls she used to be in her warm blanket, nice and cozy. While I just to sit on my chair. It was literally the best time ever. It was a daily ritual from 12:00 AM to 3:00 AM. It was just us.

After many weeks, while we were on those video calls, she was a little upset about something. When I asked her the reason she simply said nothing. But I knew there was definitely something and guess what? I was very right. She finally opened up to me and said.

"Yaddy"

"Yes, love?"

"Promise me one thing."

"Anything love."

"Never ever, leave me."

"I promise baby. No matter what we are always gonna be together, but I don't understand one thing, all of a sudden? Is anything bothering my love?"

"Mhm"

"What is it babe? Tell me each and every thing."

"So as you know we belong to different castes and I've got very conservative parents who won't accept us because of this goddamn society, how will be last forever? I am ready to go against this world but, what about my parents? I don't wanna loose them either. And of course I can't loose you."

"I understand love, but don't you worry, when I am here, all you need to fear is fear itself."

"If I betray you, I betray myself. If I betray this society, I betray my parents will. My parents will is very dear to me."

"Dearer than I?"

"No. No, not dearer than you."

She cried on the video call after this conversation of ours. We both felt emotional and very overwhelmed. She said," Yaden, I wanna marry you and live with you always. No matter what happens I want us to be together for the rest of our lives." To this we both cried that night.

Then entered the real villain of our story. Veronica. She used to sit with Ayla as her bench partner. I remember Hadric and I sat together and behind us Ayla and Veronica used to sit. Ayla and I held hands across the bench with Hadric covering us. It used to be so good, a lil risky and fun for real. Our exams were uproaching. Like the eye contacts, the 'I love you's, it was totally a surreal experience. This was the time when our exams were in a week or two, and less children came to school. Most of them, took offs for preperations.

I remember how I wrote her a love letter in class and I passed it on to Ayla through some child in the class. But unfortunately our class teacher, noticed this matter of passing on the letter and she caught it red handed. She opened the letter and read it. I was called out in class and my parents were called to school. My father got very upset and even took my phone away. It was the first time ever that I didn't talk to Ayla in so long. I could handle my parents but I was scared that what if Ayla's parents got to know about it. But thankfully nothing like that happened and I took a sigh of relief. Now since our exams were approaching we focused more on the preperations.

Our relationship was full of challenges. Not one, not two, but many. A few months before I got to know Ayla, I proposed to a girl named Olivia, it was more of an infatuation rather than love. The biggest problem was that I completely forgot about this incident and Ayla got to know it from a third person. It was a moment of betrayal of her trust for me.

Veronica dropped the biggest bomb on our lives on February 3rd. She brought out a past's memory which affected our relationship severly. She told Ayla that during our summer break somewhere in mid june, a girl kept her arm on my shoulder and we two were way more closer than we should be. Even though we were not in a relationship at that time and I had no feelings for that girl. Veronica portrayed this incident in such a manner that made Ayla feel as if her trust was completely shattered into a million pieces. From this incident onwards her trust for me was lost. So... she broke up with me. Next day, it was the biggest day of our school life. The class 10th farewell. It was a big day because most of our friends including us, could change school. And we all wanted a have a great time. Well that big day became a nightmare for us. When we reached in the school bus, I saw Veronica sittnig their with her evil smile. I confronted her and told her that she messed up everything and how she created misunderstandings between Ayla and me. I told her that it was my past and now Ayla thinks that I was at fault, all because of Veronica. I asked her to explain it to Ayla that it was my past and not something I did while I was in a relationship with Ayla. But I don't know, she didn't help me at all. That day we guys broke up and saw each other. She gave me back all the gifts I gave her, the ring, the bracelet, the pendent and most importantly the love we had for each other. That day a million promises and two hearts broke.

I can't believe everything which seemed to be perfect broke off just because of the stupidity of a third person. Well, it felt horrible. We did see each other's faces in the exams period. We did talk a little even though it felt as if the end of our world. It was our english exam and her textbook was with me. I was concerned about how she will prepare, so without wasting much time I lied at home and drove to her place which was atleast 20 kilometers away. I returned her book and...saw her. She looked as pretty as she always did.

I got to know that many rumours about Hadric and Asher were spread by none other than Kevin, who pretended to be our friend. Even Parker, added to those rumours and it got worse. The whole school bad mouthed about them both. Even though, I warned Hadric about it but at first he seemed not to care. Later, he got very conscious about it. This led to tensions between Hadric and Asher. Hadric blocked Asher and it got very serious. Later he realised his mistake and within two days, he got back with Asher. It was all because of the misunderstanding these people created between us all. But are these tensions stronger than all of our relationships and friendships? Absolutely not.

After this, Hadric told me as he got to know from Asher about Ayla and Parker's relationship. As I got to know everything about it. It felt as if someone punched my heart a million times and honestly I got so jealous. I felt as if I don't want her back anymore and now I should completely move on from her. I started to focus on myself. All my time, I used to dedicate for myself only. I started to treat my self the way I deserved. I focused on self healing and spirituality. At this point of time, I felt that I have completely moved on from her. In this attempt of self healing, I lost contact with all my friends. Even Hadric. And I was all alone.

At this time I realised that I need to take a step, immediately...

4. Reunion

Asher texted me that he got a text from Yaden. Oh.My.God how is that possible. He literally gave up on this friendship and now...nevermind. He told me how Yaden apologised to him about everything which happened between them. But honestly I was happy to see them together, better than before. It was a wholesome moment indeed. True friendship can never be lost. They may have fights, they may have tensions but they will always be back no matter what. If the friendship is real, they have to return back. So did Yaden and Asher.

"Bro, guess who texted me?"

"Who?"

"Yaden"

"Wait, what, are you serious?"

"Yes sir. He did apologise to me and now we are back. Better than before."

"Oh my god bro, tell me everything right from the start, how did it happen?"

"Okay. So basically he texted me sorry and how bad he feels about breaking that friendship off, how he realised that breaking this was never an option, communication was."

"Finally, I'm so happy for you both, bro tell me more!"

That day Asher told me everything how they both clicked back instantly as if nothing ever happened. It was such a surreal moment to see them happy together. The smile on Asher's face said everything clearly.

Asher told me everything how Yaden and him, started talking to each other more to cover the loopholes of what happened in the past. Yaden was preparing to give the IELTS exam and Asher helped him prepare for it. They started to host meetings where Asher analysed his curriculum for the exam and helped Yaden to prepare accordingly. All day they both hosted a meeting for 7 to 8 hours and discussed not only about the exam strategies but also about what's happening in their lives. It was great to see them dedicately working together. Together these guys are always unstoppable. It felt as if you know, a part of Asher has returned. The part where his heart speaks like the cosmos and his soul breathed stardust.

I asked Asher, what except from the exam strategies they discuss and he told me how they dicussed about their lives. Yaden seemed to have completely moved on from me. I felt happy for him but also...a bit empty. What I shared with Parker was love, but he was just infatuated. After he got over his lust, he left me like I never mattered. He lied to me, he deceived me and betrayed my love. I started to realise how love never demands a condition. The unconditional piece of art that breathes in the moonlight. The kind of art which requires waiting. Yaden did that art perfectly. He picked up a brush and strike a deal with his blood. He ripped open his heart for me and at this point of time I felt bad about it.

Our results were out and all of our friendgroup decided to go to school to show our results. By god's eternal grace we all scored really good grades and we went to school to meet our amazing teachers. I saw Yaden with Asher and Hadric, it was so good to see the iconic trio back. Better than before. I saw how Yaden's behaviour changed. He grew up from his past self. He did heal and I could see that in every action of his.

As I went back home, I shared with Asher a poem I wrote about love. Asher told me that Yaden would edit and post it on our new account. The old writing account was deleted by Asher to let go off the memories of the past. He said he didn't wanna hold on to them and he made this new account. I shared this poem with Asher.

She Never Knew or Did She?
I wasn't looking for love that day
just running late, bag half-zipped,
math notes flying around.
And then she—
rushing around a corridor corner,
collided into my world
with the softest crash I'll never forget.
Her eyes met mine.
Not just a glance—
a full eclipse of time,
where every sound muted
except the quiet thud of my racing heart.

From that day,
I memorized her schedule
like a sacred secret.
Timed my walks to match hers,
hoped for hallway miracles.
I knew her laugh by heart
before I knew her name.
And yet,
fear tied my words
like tangled shoelaces.
I wrote her name
in the corners of my notebooks
like a prayer.
She became
the silence in my music,
the pause in my laughter,
the reason I stayed a little longer

in places she'd just left.
Four years.
Of almost.
Of maybe.
Of what if.
And in the last pages of goodbye,
when the last bell rang
on our final day,
did I hear her say—

"I was always hoping you'd say hi."

I don't even know what came over me when I wrote those lines. Everything around me just stopped—like the world pressed pause. The noise, the rush, all of it slipped away, and all I felt was that quiet moment I tried to catch on paper.

"My fingers brushed yours gently across that book…"

I can still see it, clear as day. Feel it like it's real, like a memory I'm holding onto even if it never fully happened.

Every word was soft, like a secret meant only for someone who could hear without needing it loud. It wasn't trying to be grand or deep—it just simply was. Like how some feelings exist quietly, but so strongly you can't ignore them. Like me—trying to be brave, trying to hide what I feel, but it's still there, right beneath the surface.

I always write like that. Like the moon is lighting my way—gentle and steady.

But this time, the poem felt different. Like it wasn't just words to be read. It was something to feel, something to carry inside. That moment I tried to capture—the brush of fingers, a shared book, a glance that lasts longer than it should—it felt like magic. Simple and soft magic. The little things that don't look like much but somehow mean everything. A quiet space between two people. The hush of night. The scent of flowers. The stars just watching us.

It's just us, in that quiet.

I guess I dream honestly. Quietly. Because love doesn't always have to roar. Sometimes it's a pause. A touch that says more than words ever could.

And there's something about the way those lines hold onto someone—like telling them they're enough. Worth something real and tender, even if it's just for a moment.

Sometimes I wonder what I've done to deserve holding onto that kind of feeling. To be part of something so soft, so true.

But I want it again. Not because it's perfect or like a poem, but because I imagined it. And when you imagine something like that, it's real in a way no one else can understand.

I don't need forever.

I just want a field of flowers.

A book in our hands.

A touch that lingers.

And someone who doesn't pull away.

That's all.

If that moment ever comes—

I won't blink.

I'll just stay.

I quickly penned down so many poems about the stuff that I was going through and now Asher started his dual perspective poetry collaboration in which he wrote poems with collaborators in alternate paragraphs where both the perspectives were written and then it was edited by Yaden to be posted on our new writing account. I wrote about a fantasy of mine, where I imagined myself in a bookstore with the love of my life. I shared a picture with Asher that I found on pinterest. It was the inspiration behind his poem. I shared this poem with Asher, he added his part.

The Moment Where We Stayed

My fingers brushed yours gently across that book
I paused for a second, then I looked
I looked at your and your gaze stole my heart
The silence bloomed like a soft humming song
Like a melody of magic, nothing feels wrong
your glance, your touch, a verse I can't unread
I caressed your soul with my embrace to lead
where hearts don't follow rules, only need
To sleep in the cradle of love's gentle lullaby
Wrapped in the hush of midnight breeze
No map, no path—just you and me,
You and me, in a field full of flowers
Just us- the symphony of stars and endless hours
Wrapped in the warmth that no words can name
Forever shining in silence like how it came.

There are some moments that don't need to happen to feel real.

They arrive softly — not through footsteps, but through feeling.

Through the spaces we build inside ourselves, when the heart quietly hopes for something it never says out loud.

That's how it has always been with him.

No loud signs. No clear starts.

Just this gentle ache — not painful, but present.

Like a thought that keeps returning, always dressed in light.

Sometimes, when I'm walking through the library or brushing past a stranger in the hallway, something lingers in the air — a maybe. A possibility that tastes like stardust and stillness.

And suddenly, without trying, my mind begins to wander to a version of us the world doesn't know.

In that version, there's no fear.

No waiting.

No wondering if he notices me the way I notice him when he isn't looking.

There's only closeness.

Only calm.

Like two souls reaching toward each other in a world that finally stopped spinning.

I picture us in a room full of words, full of quiet.

His presence beside me is enough to slow time.

And even in that silence, I feel understood — like the universe wrote us into the same sentence without needing to say a word aloud.

There are no promises in this vision.

Just moments.

Moments made of glances.

Of quiet smiles.

Of the air shifting slightly when he moves his hand just close enough to mine.

I don't know why these thoughts stay with me longer than they should.

Maybe because I've always lived more in feeling than in fact.

Maybe because love, for me, has never needed to be real to be true.

And when the day ends, and the moon finds its way to my window again, I don't chase the thought away.

I let it live.

I let it breathe.

Because even if he never knows, even if it only exists here — inside me — it's still something beautiful.

And when I close my eyes, I see it clearly.

A book between us.

A soft, shared pause.

A touch that says everything we never will.

She never knew. Or maybe she did, but was just as afraid as I was. Three years of almost — of soft glances, hallway crossings, and tiny, fragile moments that never found the courage to grow into words. I still remember that one crash. The books slipping from my hands, my breath catching, and then that heartbeat… that heartbeat I tried to forget but never could. It lives inside me like a soft echo, playing every time I see someone brush past too close.

Funny, isn't it? The loudest feelings are often the ones we keep hidden — locked behind politeness, behind fear, behind everything we were told about what's possible and what's not. The way I felt never asked for much. It didn't shout. It didn't beg. It just stayed. Quiet. Soft. Constant.

I wrote his name too. In notebooks, in the margins of books, in the air when I couldn't sleep. Like a prayer. Like a secret.

Like something too sacred to say out loud. And maybe, maybe he was doing the same. Maybe our silences were speaking the same language, but we were just too afraid to listen.

What if I had just said hi? Just once. What if I had turned around, smiled, said his name like it belonged to me?

Sometimes, I wonder if love is more than just the big gestures. Maybe it's the pauses between heartbeats. The quiet between two passing steps. The warmth that lingers in a room after someone's left. Maybe love lives in the "what ifs" — the ones that sting, not because they're lost, but because they were never given a chance to live.

I don't know what would've happened if I had reached out. Maybe we would've bloomed. Maybe we would've burned. But sometimes, I think the saddest part isn't the ending — it's never getting to start.

Still, in the silence of some nights, when the world hushes just enough, I imagine. I imagine a moment that didn't happen but could've. A moment where the world stopped, where fingers brushed, and hearts didn't hold back. Where there was no map, no fear, just us — two souls pausing in a world too loud.

And maybe that's what love is, too. I wrote something with Asher about eye contacts. There's this thing about eye contacts which just steals us a moment. Asher and I always shared a platonic bond, just two

poetic hearts writing poetry. It was like he never knew the fact that I knew he wrote everything from Yaden's perspective.He gave words to Yaden's heart. Anyways, I shared with him a poem about another deliberation where love traces my path.

WHISPERED IN THE SUNLIT HAZE

In silent strands our stories lie,
Untied within whispers, passes by
Beneath the stars, beneath the sky
Wrapping the secrets with smiles so shy.
her laughter rings, a soft disguise
Into the echoes of her sweet surprise
She dreams in verses, bold yet shy
She writes love with a look in her eye
She walks through days with the quiet grace
When her charm meets desire, a lovely solace

A heart alight in the sunlit haze— as the world may see her gentle gaze.
A soul rewritten by the stars held aloft-
Embedded in love she holds so soft!

I don't think he ever truly knew how much those small moments meant to me.

It wasn't a love story, not in the way people write them. There were no confessions under moonlight, no dramatic promises. Just… glances. Quiet ones. The kind that lingered a little too long behind the school stage during lunch breaks. The kind where the whole world stood still — like even time wanted to eavesdrop on what our eyes were saying.

I remember that one lunch — the way he sat next to me, like it was the most natural thing. He didn't ask, and I didn't mind. Our knees brushed and neither of us moved. He offered me half his sandwich, and I gave him the last bite of mine — the one I usually saved. We didn't speak much. We didn't need to.

It's strange how those silent moments carry more weight than a thousand words.

Behind that stage, where the world couldn't see us, I felt more seen than ever. Our hands touched once — by accident or maybe not. And he didn't pull away. Neither did I. We just stayed there, fingertips brushing, like two people unsure whether they're allowed to want more.

Sometimes, we'd bump into each other in the hallway — messy, unplanned moments that left my heart racing. I'd act casual. He'd smile a little. Our shoulders would meet for a second longer than needed. And when we passed each other, I'd turn back… and sometimes, he already was.

I don't know why I never said anything.

Maybe I was scared to break whatever fragile thing we were holding — or scared to find out it was never real for him. But God, the way he looked at me sometimes… it felt like poetry. Like he knew something I didn't, or maybe something we both were too scared to admit.

There was a day — I still remember — when we stood inches apart, tucked away between the art room and the stairwell. It was quiet. Everyone else was at lunch. And for a moment, we just looked at each other. No noise. No one watching. Just two people, standing in the middle of a story they never started but already felt a part of.

That eye contact... it was everything. It told me he knew. That I knew. That maybe, in another world — or maybe just one moment of courage — we would've been something more.

But even if we never speak of it…

Even if all we had were glances, brushes, and shared bites of lunch...

It was enough to write poems about.

It was enough to make silence feel full.

And maybe... just maybe...

One day we will find each other.

Suddenly I received a text from Asher.

"Hi bro, how are you liking the collaborations so far?"

"I must say bro, they all are stunning."

"Well let me tell you something, they all have been edited by Yaden and I must say, his song preferences...are definitely on the point."

"Yeah...correct. They definitely are."

"Yes and you know what, the other day he also told me that it was his favourite song."

"Wait. But it is the same song that I recommended him while we were dating."

"Really?"

"Mhm."

"You see songs...music,art and poetry, these are soul

connections and can't let us forget some moments."

"Yup, you're very right bro!"

That day I realised that no matter where we go, or where we are, but we will always be connected through our souls. I read about this Chinese theory about the red string of fate. Those who are connected by the souls, they are forever tied within the invisible red thread of love. It does not break. It does not remain visible. But it is always there. And it is just like love which doesn't need to be shown or proved daily but just make us feel alive.

"Bro, can I ask you something casually if you don't mind?"

"Yeah bro definitely go ahead."

"Don't get me wrong but do you still have some sort of feelings for Yaden?"

"No like I do not have any feelings for him."

"Okay so basically do you want him as a friend?"

"Yes, I have told you many times that I always enjoyed his company, not gonna lie."

"Yes I definitely remember you saying that."

"You know what, at this point of time I don't even know what I want."

"You definitely miss him, don't you?"

"Mhm."

"What if I tell you that you can always text him and have him back?"

"Bro but he will not accept me now, it's very late and I don't know."

"And what makes you think that?"

"After all what I did with him, I don't think so that he is going to come back with me."

"Okay listen what if I tell you that you people are just one text away?"

"Really, can it happen?"

"Yes, yes why not. Do you want me to ask him?"

"Okay bro go on will you know how to do this conversation right."

Asher texts Yaden and he talks about this whole matter with him. Yaden was very happy and overwhelmed after listening to this whole conversation which happened between me and Asher. After all, he also wanted us back and we both grew up better than before. We both were now enough to understand that love can never stop us from wanting to have each other back. I had a call with Asher regarding all this, he told me how Yaden was sceptical and didn't want to get his heart broken again. He also told me that Yaden felt nervous to make the first move. So was I. So Asher decided to make a group chat again like we use to have 2 years ago. He made the group and we all started to text in it. Yaden was so genuinely happy, that he couldn't stop thanking Asher. After all we had a great role in our whole journey. Later we all text a lot in that group chat. After a few hours as Asher went to sleep. We talked in the personal messages about our whole journey of separation and how we used to miss us.

That night, we texted each other for so long until we get our hearts together again. We both had a very overwhelming conversation and from the next day onwards I also joined the meeting between Yaden and Asher, as the both discussed about the IELTS exam preparation and strategies, and talked about their daily lives and everything, I also joined them and Yaden and I had a wholesome conversation with deep talks and chit chat sessions between Asher, Yaden and me. From countless jokes to endless discussions, I felt as if all of us, were now truly back. Today I could finally say that we have attend peace.

The war is over.

Later after few days we decided to have a visit to the nearest mall to watch a cinematic movie. We did all this so that Yaden and I could spend more time together, and in this attempt we all can relax and enjoy yourself as our exams got over recently. It was literally the best day ever. We planned the whole day in advance.

The whole day consisted of- Yaden, Asher, Hardic, Sienna and I. We also had two more friends who accompanied us. At first we played many games and Yaden got me a keychain as a price which he won from the games.

Later we enjoyed clicking a lot of good pictures together. Asher clicked thousands of pictures of Yaden and me. Each and every single picture was very well clicked and Yaden even set one of our pictures in which we were looking towards each other as the wallpaper of his phone.

"Yaddy!"

"Yes, love?"

"What's the password of your phone?"

"What's your birth date?"

"Oh my god, you did not-"

"Yes I did."

"I love you so much!"

"I love you too babygirl!"

After a while we also ate some good food. And when we were about to leave the mall while booking our cabs to go home, Yaden gifted me a pair of my favourite earrings that I casually mentioned while talking to him. I literally felt so happy then I couldn't express my feelings in mere words. It was the best feeling in the whole world, I was feeling as if I am on the top of the moon. Also while were watching the movie we held hands the entire time. As Asher and Hardic went down to buy some snacks during the interval, I kissed Yaden on his cheek. He blushed like a rose.

Red and charming.

I love this guy so much.

Oh my god.

I came across a poem, that Asher wrote long about..."Just Friends". I sent it to Yaden as if reading it to him.

But before I did, I stared at it for what felt like hours.

Each line, each rhyme, each little breath of confession—I read it slowly, like I was peeling away my own excuses. The words weren't mine, but they spoke like they'd been stolen from the corners of my mind. They weren't addressed to me, but they fit like a glove I had been hiding behind for too long.

It was maddening.

Because I had said it first. "Let's just be friends."

That had been my sentence. My shield. My script.

Not because I didn't feel something, but because I did.

Because I felt too much.

And the more I read Asher's poem, the more I realized it mirrored the space between what I said and what I meant. It was the quiet grief of having something beautiful within reach, and pretending it was nothing more than casual. Comfortable. Contained.

I never meant to lie.

But the truth? It was messy. Scary. It had no script.

So I did what I knew—I named it friendship and hoped my heart would eventually believe me.

It never did.

So now, I found myself staring at this poem, this confession soaked in rhythm and regret, thinking of all the things I never told Yaden. I said that I want him as a friend but the truth is we could never be, "Just Friends". We are meant to be forever.

HONEYMOON

You said we are just friends but you look me in the eye,
Oh boy how your eyes danced dreamily into my sky.
Tell me that you love me with all the waves in my ocean blue eyes,
Stop telling 'we're just friends', Oh how beautifully you lie!

You said we're just friends but something in you denies
The fact that you're not jealous seeing someone who tries
To get me in their eyes and to make me realise
That I'm better off with them which even my heart defies.
You said we're just friends but with me you get those butterflies
Reigning the realm of your stomach which tickles and ties
The threads of love a bit too tighter as your heart sighs
That a part of you is obsessed with me, oh boy when you'd realise.
You said we're just friends but grab my waist tight,
Kiss my cheeks coming down to my lips even right,
Can't forget when you said,"Lift your hips for me, love." that night,
Where I tie your body with my hugs and you said, "Ignite, my love, Ignite."

I don't know how to explain it.

It wasn't something grand or loud or dramatic — it was just… right.

Like the way sunsets don't need permission to be beautiful, or how rain sometimes falls only to remind the earth how much it missed the sky.

That day at the mall — it's still playing in my head like a favourite scene from a movie I never want to end. And maybe it wasn't anything crazy — just us, our friends, a movie, some laughter, a keychain, and the softest pair of hands I've ever held — but for me, it was everything.

It felt like all those little wishes I whispered at 11:11 were heard. Slowly. Gently. In his voice, in his smile, in the way he looked at me when I wasn't even looking at him.

There was something in that day that felt like a sigh of relief — like the universe finally exhaled and said, "Here, you can rest now. You're safe."

When he set our picture — the one where we were looking at each other — as his wallpaper, something shifted inside me. Not loudly. Not dramatically. Just… a quiet confirmation. That maybe love doesn't need to be loud to be real.

And when I asked him for his phone password and he said my birthdate?

God. My heart.

My heart didn't know whether to scream, cry, or melt.

I just kept thinking: This is it. This is what it feels like to be someone's favourite person.

Not in a forced way. Not because I asked for it. But because he chose to make it that way.

I remember how my earrings sparkled under the mall lights when he gave them to me — the ones I mentioned so casually, without even thinking. I didn't expect him to remember. But he did. And not only that — he went out of his way to get them.

That's when I knew.

That love isn't always in the grand gestures. Sometimes it's tucked into memories. In someone who listens even when you think they're not.

We held hands the whole movie. And I kissed him on the cheek. He blushed like the softest shade of rose. I swear, in that moment, he looked like something God must've carved with extra care.

And maybe this is what love is supposed to feel like — not loud, but full. Not perfect, but present. Not fairy tale, but something better.

Real.

And right now, I wouldn't trade this feeling for the whole universe.

Because I have him.

And that's all the magic I'll ever need.

The amount of love I have for him is unmatchable. I want him for the rest of my life. Oh my god, please, this time protect our relationship. If forever feels like being in his arms, then burn me alive, and let his name be the flame.

At the end of the day, It was us. Just us...

Letter to Ayla

My dearest Ayla,

I don't know where to begin, and I suppose that's the truest sign of how much I've missed you — how words fumble in the face of emotions too large to name. Yet here I am, in a new country, under a different sky, with you still occupying every part of me.

Sometimes, I look out the window of my flat in the UK and imagine you walking down the street below — your hair catching the wind, your eyes searching for mine, and that half-smile curling at your lips when you finally see me. I imagine us here, not just in love, but together — the kind of togetherness we were denied for far too long.

You know, Ayla, I often think about everything we went through. The nights when we lay on opposite ends of the city, clutching our phones like lifelines, whispering promises into screens that could never quite hold the warmth of a real touch. The people who tried — so hard — to pull us apart. The ones who couldn't stand the kind of love we shared because they never knew something so tender could also be so strong. But fate, as always, had other plans. And I believe it always did.

When everything felt like it was crumbling, when even I started doubting whether love could survive so much strain, it was your

memory that held me together. It was those quiet moments —
bumping into each other in the school hallway, laughing over
stolen snacks, your fingers brushing against mine — that
reminded me that we were not temporary. We were meant.

Asher and Hadric... God, I owe them more than words. When I
was falling apart, when everything around me seemed like noise,
they were the calm. It was Asher who sat beside me with IELTS
books, day after day, reminding me why I needed to keep going.
He never let me give up, not even on the days I wanted to lock
myself away and forget the world existed. And Hadric — he was
the one who reminded me of you. He kept slipping your name
into conversations, dropping memories of the times we all spent
together, bringing you to life even in your absence. They didn't
just help me pass that exam. They helped me believe in something
again.

Now that I'm here — fully settled, with a job, a small but cozy
apartment, and a growing life — I want one thing more than
anything else: you.

I miss everything. I miss your earrings that glimmered when you
laughed too hard. I miss the way you would roll your eyes at my
terrible jokes and then laugh anyway. I miss the way you hugged
me from behind when I was too lost in my thoughts. I miss the
way your presence made the air lighter, the world brighter, and my

heart quieter.

Well, Ayla — I'm building it. It's not perfect, and I still have nights when I feel lonely in a room full of people. But I'm working hard, every day, to create a space that feels like home. And it won't truly be home until you're here.

So, this is more than a love letter. It's a request. A dream. A hope. I want you to come here. Not just to visit, not just to see this new life, but to become a part of it. I want us to walk hand in hand down unfamiliar streets and make them ours. I want to cook dinner with you in this tiny kitchen, fight over which movie to watch, kiss you in the quiet corners of this place we now share. I want to wake up next to you, marry you under the soft sun of this new city, and write the rest of our story with peace, not pain.

I miss you with a kind of ache I can't describe. I miss your voice in the mornings and your "good night" texts. I miss your presence in my memories and your promise in my future. And even though this letter can't carry the full weight of my love, I hope it reaches you as a whisper of everything I want to say in person.

Ayla, please come.

There's a space beside me in this world I'm building, and it has always belonged to you.

Also I am missing Hardic and Asher so much, I need them here with me. And of course you, my love. I wonder when you guys will be here. I remember you told me how you will come here after your Bachelors in Science gets completed. I remember, Asher telling me that he will come here after his Masters in English Literature to pursue his PhD. And when he comes Asher and Hardic, both of them can come together. I have so much to say, a lot more, when you come here with me. Till then I am always waiting for you people...

Forever yours,

Yaden

P.S. Tell me when you're coming, and I'll be waiting at the airport with your favorite flowers. Don't keep me waiting too long. I love you...

The Flight

"They say flight, is a metaphor for escape. I rebel that it is a metaphor for separation."

In the bloom of a season when stars used to sing,
Two hearts danced gently beneath love's wing.
Fingers entwined like verses and rhyme,
Laughter was easy, and so was time.

Hallways held secrets, slow hands, and grace,
Notes in a locker, a soft warm embrace.
A look, a smile, the silence they shared,
In their little universe, they knew they were paired.

But winds grew restless, and rumors took flight,
Shadows arrived, stealing the light.
Words became thorns, and silence grew loud,
They drifted apart, lost in a crowd.

Best friends tried—truly, they tried,
They stitched the stars the heartbreaks untied.
But fate was stubborn, and time wasn't kind,
Love became something they both left behind.

The boy once bold grew quiet and still,
Learning to heal by force of will.

He studied the skies with a tired gaze,
And learned to dream in disciplined ways.

He soared on papers, cleared every test,
Packed up his hopes, left behind the rest.
Two best friends waved from the terminal gate,
As love wore a locket engraved with fate.

Now oceans whisper what once was near,
And time zones stretch between "I'm here."
She stands with memories stitched in gold,
Of gifts once given, of hands she'd hold.

But love's not a thing that distance can drown,
It grows, it lingers, it circles around.
For even when miles make moments seem small,
Love still answers when memories call.

He writes her letters in midnight's hue,
Each word a promise, steadfast and true.
"Wait for me, love, till the stars realign,
We missed the spring, but the fall can be mine."

A flight is just steel, engines, and air,
But for them, it's a prayer said anywhere.
For once they were close but falling apart,
Now they're afar but closer in heart.

One day, she'll board with trembling grace,
And find him waiting in foreign place.
He'll hold her like poems, like rain, like sun—
The chapter they dreamed has just begun.

Letter to Yaden

My dearest Yaden,

Your letter—oh God, your letter.

I must have read it a hundred times before I could even think of replying. The way your words found me... it was like being held again, like being seen after so long. You have no idea how much I needed you in that moment. And somehow, you arrived—through ink, through paper, through the wind.

You miss me, and my whole heart aches because I miss you too—so much that sometimes I feel like I carry an invisible version of you around me all day. I miss your laughter, the way it rises in little waves before crashing into my chest. I miss how you always knew what to say when I didn't know how to be okay. I miss the small things—the way you'd take my hand without thinking, how your eyes searched mine before speaking, like you always wanted to be sure I was still here.

I am still here, Yaden. I never left—not really. Even when we were apart, even when words failed, even when oceans and years tried to break us, a part of me was always rooted in you.

And now, reading your words, I feel that part waking up again.

I'm so proud of you. Of how far you've come. Of how you've kept your heart intact, even when the world gave you every reason to harden it. I can feel your strength in every line, but I can also feel the softness. The softness you never lost. The softness you still offer me.

You said there's a space beside you that still belongs to me.
I know that space.
I've missed it more than I can put into words.

I imagine it often. Sitting beside you at the windowsill, legs tangled, your shoulder against mine. Talking about everything and nothing. Just being. And you—looking at me with that smile that isn't really a smile but something else entirely. Something only I ever understood.

You mentioned Asher. I remember him being so gentle when you needed that the most. And I know how much he misses you too. It's easy to tell, even through the distance. Hadric does too—his silence says more than words sometimes. I can feel how much the three of you have held each other together. It gives me peace to know you haven't been alone. And I promise, when I come, I'll step into this life of yours with all the respect and care it deserves.

I'm coming after completing my Bachelor's in Science — and it feels like I've carried the thought of you with me through every exam, every lecture, every late night I spent wondering where this path would lead. Asher, too, is on his way; he'll be coming after completing his Master's in English Literature. He's so passionate, Yaden — I wish you could've seen the way his eyes lit up every time he read something that reminded him of you. He's planning to pursue his PhD abroad, and we all know he's going to be brilliant. There's even talk of Hadric joining him later; I can already imagine the two of them walking through old libraries in foreign cities, their laughter echoing between the shelves. We all miss you — more than words, more than time, more than distance. And when we're all together again, we're going to live a little louder. We've made plans, you know — wild, silly, beautiful plans. To travel, to see places none of us have seen, to dance at night on empty streets, to take photos that look like they belong in old books, and to remind ourselves that we're still young, still dreaming, still alive. We want to be successful — not just in careers, but in meaning. We want lives filled with purpose, poetry, and the kind of love that never fades. And you, Yaden… you're the center of all that. You always were.

But above all, Yaden, I'm coming for you.

There's something I need to tell you. And I can't keep it from you anymore.

I'm coming to the UK. Really. Not next year. Not later. Not someday.

Soon.

And no—I won't tell you when.

I want it to be a moment. Our moment.
You'll see me at the airport. Or maybe you'll turn a corner and there I'll be, standing with that scarf you once teased me about, eyes searching for the boy I never stopped loving.
And you'll know.

And I'll run to you.
And you'll hold me.
And all of this distance will collapse.

No more waiting. No more what-ifs.
Just us—finally.

You once told me that the moon looked different when I wasn't around.
Let's fix that.

You said love isn't just a feeling—it's a decision. A return. A choosing.

Well, I'm choosing you. Again. And again. And again.

Always yours,

Ayla

P.S. I'll be wearing those earrings you love—the ones that always swing when I laugh. Make me laugh, Yaden. I've waited long enough.

The Arrival

"They say arrival, is a metaphor of ending. I rebel that it is a
metaphor for beginings."

They say arrival is a metaphor for closure.

I rebel.

Arrival is not the end — it is the return of breath.

It is the trembling pause

before the first step into a dream long starved.

It is the heart, rising —

not to finish something,

but to begin again.

I wrote today's date slowly,

as if my hands feared the ink might betray the truth.

As if by writing it,

I could summon all the softness this moment deserved.

It had been years,

not in time —

but in ache.

And still,

each second away had carved letters in my bones,

silent syllables of longing

I could never quite whisper out loud.

The day of your return
came not with thunder —
but with sky.

There was no dramatic rain, no cinematic music —
just the hush of a city holding its breath
as your name floated through air like a forgotten prayer.

I watched the terminal with the stillness of someone
who'd spent too long holding onto air.
And when you appeared —
no fireworks exploded.
Just my soul.
Silently. Entirely.
Like the tide surrendering to the moon
after lifetimes of resistance.

You walked as though the earth had remembered you.
And I—
I stood still, afraid one blink might dissolve you back into
memory.

When your eyes found mine,
it was not recognition.
It was resurrection.
My God,
how long had I been waiting to feel alive like this?

We didn't run to each other.
We simply… arrived.
Like rivers meeting at last.
Like all the unsaid things curling in our throats
and choosing, at last, to breathe.

You looked changed —
but only in the way stars look older
when you love them more.
And you spoke of distant cities,
of degrees earned and dreams planted,
of cold mornings and lonely libraries.
I listened not to your words,
but to the pauses in between —
the quiet aching you tried to hide,
the echo of my name I knew lived in your every silence.

And when I told you I had waited,
you didn't believe me.
But then again,
only someone who had also waited
could recognize that kind of truth in the eyes.

We wandered through the old streets
that once echoed our laughter,
each building still remembering our footsteps.

You said you missed the sky here.
I said the sky missed you too.

We spoke of futures —
of further studies, of borders we'd still cross.
You dreamed of learning in lands far away,
and I, selfish in love, still smiled.
Because love does not cage.
Love is the wind in your sail,
even when you sail far from its shore.

You said another might join you, someday —
someone who shared your fire, your purpose.
And I nodded,
knowing that the ones who walk beside you
will never replace the one who waited.

And just as twilight folded into the arms of the night,
laughter emerged.
Familiar.
Unmistakable.

They came —
not like thunder, but like memory.
Their voices tumbled into the air like old songs,
filling spaces we didn't know were still empty.
They came with jokes half-finished,

stories half-true,

and hearts fully open.

No grand reunions.

Just clumsy hugs.

Too-long-held tears.

And silence so full, it didn't need to be filled.

We sat beneath the same sky

we once wished upon,

and no one had to ask if this moment was enough.

It was more than enough.

It was everything.

The stars didn't shine brighter —

we simply noticed them more.

Because that's what happens

when the ones you love are finally home.

We will go places now.

We will carry dreams and fears and stardust in our pockets.

We will grow and stumble, and still —

we will return.

To this.

To each other.

Because the greatest journeys
do not end with arrivals.
They begin with them.

And in this soft, golden moment —
we have all arrived.

Epilouge

And Then, the Moon Smiled Back

The stars had shifted. Not in the careless way one turns their face to avoid a gaze, but in the way lovers realign themselves in a crowded room—quietly, purposefully, with a gravity no eye could ignore. It was as if the entire universe had been waiting for this very moment: not for the arrival of a plane, but for the arrival of a promise. A promise held tight in years of distance and silence, a promise that now began to take shape again beneath the gentle, knowing smile of the moon.

Ayla was the first to step down onto the ground she had missed so deeply—the familiar cracked pavement of the airport's arrival hall, the faint scent of rain mingled with city dust, the distant hum of cars and the murmur of voices flowing like a tide. The soles of her shoes whispered softly against the floor, cautious but sure. The wind did not roar or scatter leaves as it often did; instead, it sighed—a quiet breath, as though it, too, had been holding itself together until this very moment.

She was not the same girl who had left all those months ago. Time had carved sharper edges on her soul, education had inked her thoughts with the colors of science and reason, but love—that steadfast force—had kept her whole, unbroken. She returned not just with a degree, or a collection of certificates, but with the certainty that love, when honest and consistent, was stronger than any doubt, distance, or decay. It was a truth she had learned the hard way, a lesson written in the margins of lonely nights and fleeting calls.

Across the vast hall, a presence stirred. Taller than she remembered, quieter than she had imagined, yet somehow more complete—Yaden. His eyes, when they found hers, held a depth that seemed carved from the same stardust as her own. The moment stretched and folded around them like a delicate dance, slow and sacred.

They say arrival is a metaphor for reunion, but Ayla had come to believe differently. Arrival was not reunion—it was resurrection. It was the rebirth of something that had never truly died.

All the whispers and warnings she had heard before—how he would forget her, how she would outgrow him, how time would carve them separate—had melted away like stars fading into dawn. Because what no one understood was that real love does not simply vanish. It delays, it detours, but it never dies. It plants itself deep in the soul, like moonlight glistening still on restless ocean waves—silent, steady, and glowing with its own timeless light.

Yaden walked towards her with a calm surety. No words passed between them—only a breath shared, a single, fragile moment where the ache of all the years apart crashed into the flood of finally being able to touch again.

And Ayla, too, remained silent. For some arrivals do not need words. They need silence, to echo what absence had screamed for far too long.

Their fingers found each other—tentative, searching—then intertwined like roots seeking earth after a storm. Their silence was louder than any song, deeper than any poem. Their stillness contained a universe held between two heartbeats. They stood like poetry, unrhymed yet somehow perfectly complete.

Time bent around them. The airport faded away like mist. People became mere watercolor silhouettes. All that remained was the radiant presence of two souls finally home.

And then, a soft murmur of laughter escaped Ayla's lips. It was the kind of laugh that dances lightly on eyelashes, born not from humor, but from survival—from knowing that love had been tested by silence, loneliness, and time, and had passed every exam.

Later, they found a quiet corner by a small bench, each cradling a paper cup of chai, the steam rising in gentle curls between them. Ayla told him about the stars she had studied—the atoms that reminded her of him, tiny and infinite all at once. Yaden spoke of books that missed her in their margins, windows that refused to open because her touch lingered on their glass.

They did not have to say, "I missed you." It was in the way their hands refused to let go, the way her head tilted into his shoulder like it had been shaped for that very moment, the way his breath slowed only when she exhaled.

Their days became sacred again. Mornings were shared silences, where the warmth of the rising sun on their faces was enough dialogue. Afternoons unfolded as rediscovery—wandering through old cafés still scented with cinnamon and vanilla, bookstores that held the same rustling secrets in their pages. Evenings carried the tenderness of dreams spoken aloud, and nights whispered back what home truly meant: each other.

Yaden began slipping little notes into the pages of her books again—folded corners, soft scribbles like "You are my quiet in the chaos," or "Your absence made the moon dim." Ayla returned the gesture, sketching molecules that bloomed into stars, drawn in the margins of his worn journals.

One afternoon, they unearthed an old photograph from their early days—a frozen moment in time. Ayla, with wild hair and eyes full of hope. Yaden, awkward and impossibly kind. They laughed until tears spilled, not from nostalgia, but from survival—from knowing that they had grown together, even through distance.

The love they carried now was no longer just young and poetic—it was weathered and wise. It had endured winters without warmth, monsoons of doubt, and still, like a rare flower, it had bloomed with fierce beauty.

Their friends came soon after.

Yaden had seen many people arrive at the airport before. First it was him, then a few years later, Ayla came after finishing her degree. But nothing felt like this moment—when Asher and Hadríc finally arrived. The airport doors slid open like they always did, but to Yaden, it felt like time itself had paused. Asher came out first. He looked more grown up, with tired eyes and the calmness of someone who had read too many books. The moment he saw Yaden, he dropped his bag and walked straight into his arms. Their hug was quiet, full of feeling. "You've no idea how much I've missed this," Asher whispered. Yaden's voice shook as he replied, "I waited all these years."

Then Hadríc walked in, grinning like he always did, but his eyes showed emotion too. Without a word, he joined the hug, wrapping his arms around both of them. And just like that, the trio was whole again. Hadríc's hug was full of energy and comfort, like a wave of joy. "You still smell like cheap perfume and old books," he joked, and they all laughed with tears in their eyes.

The three of them stood there, surrounded by suitcases and strangers, but in their own little world. They weren't just school friends anymore—they were grown up, changed by time, distance, and life. But in that moment, with arms around each other and memories rushing back, they felt like nothing had changed. They were home again, together.

Asher, with his overflowing journals and dreams tangled in metaphor, returned from his corridors of English literature, clutching a PhD application. Hadric , with music stitched in his fingers and rebellion dancing in his smile.

They reunited not as strangers but as constellations reassembling the same sky—each star familiar and bright. Their laughter was louder now, carrying the weight of every tear shed in years of silence. They teased one another, argued over playlists, and sat in cafés where chairs still remembered their teenage selves.

One night, they wandered barefoot through the empty corridors of their old school. Asher's fingers traced the dusty lockers, Hadríc's voice hummed quiet melodies into the hollow halls. Yaden lingered at the back of the classroom where he had first glimpsed Ayla, and Ayla, eyes shining with galaxies, whispered, "This is where it all began."

The school seemed smaller now, but their memories had grown larger—brighter, more vivid.

There was a late-night picnic beneath a nearly full moon. Stories spilled like honey, voices overlapping in a chaotic harmony where no one's voice was lost. Ayla wrapped herself in her favorite scarf. Asher read his unfinished poem aloud. Hadríc sang half a chorus, enough to send laughter rippling through the air. Yaden looked around at them all, and knew: this was the arrival the world had been waiting for.

It was not a moment.

It was the dawn of an era.

They were not the same anymore.

They were stronger.

They had survived the cruelties of comparison, the whispers of gossip, the misunderstandings, and the endless years when all they had were typed words and unanswered calls.

But look at them now—

Together.

Unbreakable.

Unshakeable.

Unfolding.

Love had not just returned.

It had arrived.

And from high above, the moon smiled back.

The Morning After

The next morning, dawn seeped gently into the room, casting pale gold across their faces. Ayla awoke with the soft weight of

Yaden's hand resting over hers, their fingers still entwined like they'd been molded for each other.

She traced the delicate lines of his palm, memorizing every crease as if it were a map back to the past and a path toward the future.

They sat by the window, watching the world begin again—the slow stir of life in the city below, the flutter of leaves in the morning breeze. Ayla's thoughts drifted over the months they had lost, the silence that had stretched between them like a canyon.

Yet here they were—on the other side.

She smiled quietly to herself, the certainty settling deep within her: love was not just a feeling, but a revolution. It defied time, healed wounds, and created new constellations out of old scars.

They spoke of dreams—plans to chase, to explore, to build something lasting. Not just a relationship, but a shared life, stitched together with patience and trust.

Yaden looked at her with a tenderness that made her heart swell. "We have so much to learn," he said softly. "But I'm ready. With you."

Ayla nodded, the moonlight from last night still shimmering in her veins.

Together, they stepped out into the waking world, knowing the universe had already begun to dance around their promise.

Under the Vast Sky

Days turned into weeks, and their reunion blossomed into a deeper understanding. They learned to navigate the changes—the new layers of themselves, the lessons carved by absence.

In quiet moments, Ayla would catch Yaden staring at the night sky, eyes reflecting the constellations they once dreamed beneath.

"Do you think the stars remember us?" she asked one evening.

He smiled, brushing a stray hair from her face. "They do. Because they've seen our story written in light."

Sometimes they walked along the riverbank, watching the moon's reflection ripple in the water. Their conversations floated like gentle currents—sometimes weighty, sometimes playful, always real.

Their friends became family again. Asher's poetry deepened, weaving their shared history into words that danced with fire. Hadríc's music became a soundtrack to their lives—rebellious and tender, wild and true.

Together, they formed a constellation not just of friendship, but of resilience and hope.

The Promise

One evening, beneath a sky heavy with stars, Yaden took Ayla's hand once more.

"This," he said, voice steady but soft, "is our forever. Not because we never stumble, but because we rise again. Together."

Ayla looked up at the moon, shining brighter than ever.

And smiled back.

Because this time, their love was not just a promise—it was a home.

The moon hung low that night, bathing the world in silver—like a witness to their unspoken vows. Ayla traced constellations in the sky with her fingers, as if drawing invisible bridges from her heart to theirs. Yaden caught her hand and held it close, feeling the pulse of years that had both separated and stitched them back together.

"Do you remember," Ayla whispered, "how we used to sneak out from the dorms to stare at the night sky? Like the stars knew all our secrets."

Yaden smiled, the memory a warm ember inside him. "I think they still do. And maybe they've been waiting to tell us the rest."

The friends leaned back on the soft grass, the night cradling their silence like a lullaby. There was a sacredness to the moment — a stillness that only years of waiting and hoping can create.

They spoke of dreams once paused and now rekindled. Of the bittersweet edges of growing up. Of the places they'd gone, the people they'd become.

Asher spoke quietly about poetry that could hold the world's pain and still make you believe in dawn.

Hadríc hummed a new melody that carried the ache and joy of youth, promising songs that would last beyond their time.

Ayla looked at them all and felt the tides of love and friendship pull her back to the girl who had once stood scared but hopeful beneath the same moon.

Yaden squeezed her hand softly, as if to say: here, in this constellation of souls, you are home.

Echoes of Eternity

Days turned to weeks, and their lives began to weave together again—not seamlessly, but with the beautiful imperfections of things lived fully. They took turns cooking meals in cramped apartments, studied together beneath flickering lamps, and debated fiercely about everything from politics to poetry.

The bond between Ayla and Yaden grew quietly deeper. The small notes in books evolved into letters—long, handwritten letters that smelled faintly of rain and ink. In one letter, Ayla wrote:

"Love is no longer just the moonlight on water. It's the water itself—sometimes calm, sometimes stormy, but always real."

Yaden responded with a poem tucked into an old book:

"If I could rewrite the stars, I would make sure they spell your name in every sky."

Their love was no longer the reckless blaze of youth, but a steady flame—patient, enduring, and warm.

Forever, yours...

One afternoon, beneath a sky that threatened rain, they visited the small park where they had once carved their initials into an old oak tree. The bark was rough now, scarred by time and weather, but the initials remained.

They sat on the bench nearby, hands entwined, watching the first drops fall.

Ayla smiled softly. "I think some things survive storms better than we expect."

Yaden nodded. "Because they're rooted deep."

Heartbeat

The reunion of friends blossomed into shared adventures. They traveled to the hills where the air smelled of pine and possibility, sat around bonfires that crackled with stories and laughter, and chased dawns along empty beaches.

Everywhere they went, the moon seemed to follow—sometimes a crescent shyly peeking, sometimes a glowing orb lighting their paths. It was as if the cosmos celebrated their resilience.

In quiet moments, Ayla would close her eyes and feel the steady beat of Yaden's heart next to hers—a rhythm that had traveled across distance and time to become their shared song.

Growth

Their circle of friends expanded with time—new faces, new stories, but always that thread of constellations connecting them. There was Asher, who found beauty in broken words; Hadríc, whose melodies could heal; Ayla, whose science had become a language of wonder; and Yaden, whose steady presence was the anchor to their skies.

Together, they learned that arrival wasn't a single moment, but a journey marked by resilience, forgiveness, and unwavering hope.

Tapestry of twilight

One evening, as twilight wrapped the city in violet and gold, Ayla and Yaden stood on a rooftop overlooking the skyline. The moon was full, radiant—a perfect orb of light.

Ayla whispered, "Do you think the moon ever gets lonely up there, watching us from so far away?"

Yaden pulled her close, their shadows blending into one. "Maybe. But I think it smiles because it knows we've found each other again."

The city lights flickered below like distant stars, and for a moment, everything felt infinite.

Golden dot

Months later, Ayla found herself standing before a crowd—her first lecture after returning home, her voice steady and sure. She spoke not only of atoms and stars but of love and resilience—the kind that survives time and distance, that refuses to be erased by silence. She thought about the childhood love wher Yaden once told him," You are the golden dot of mine, that I will identify in every crowd."

Yaden watched from the back, pride shining in his eyes, knowing that this was only the beginning of their story's next chapter.

Constellations of love

Their love was no longer just a quiet echo beneath the moon. It was a roaring flame, a constellation bright enough to guide others through their own darkness.

Because true love, they had learned, is never just about arrival.

It is about the courage to keep coming back.

To keep choosing.

To keep lighting the night.

Better together

And so, beneath the watchful gaze of the moon, Ayla and Yaden—and their constellation of friends—stepped boldly into the future.

Together.

Unbreakable.

Forever unfolding.

The moon smiled back, and the stars whispered their blessings...

Letter From The Author's Desk

Dearest Readers,

I don't know where to begin. I never do.

I think I've always been better at endings.

At last pages. At final gazes. At the kind of goodbyes that don't echo, but burn.

But here I am again…

Seventeen, still trying to translate emotions into ink.

This is my third book.

It's not The Laureate of Moonlit Dreams.

It's not 18 Epiphanies of the Moon.

This is something else entirely.

This is a scream disguised as a whisper.

This is the moonlight that poured out of me when everything else refused to stay.

I didn't write this to impress.

I wrote this because I had no choice.

Because grief doesn't ask for permission.

Because sometimes, poetry is the only place where I still feel whole.

This book—An Ode to Celestial Romanticism—is everything I am and everything I'm scared to become.

It is part essay, part poem, part fiction, part memory, part mistake.

It's the letter I never sent.

The hug I never gave.

The version of myself I buried to survive.

You'll find stories here that were never meant to be stories.

Just real moments, dressed in stardust, aching to be remembered.

One in particular—you'll feel it—comes from a real place.

My best friend. His love.

Their love wasn't perfect.

It was real.

And it made me believe in something again.

Not happily ever afters.

But honestly ever nows.

They reminded me that love doesn't always look like roses and rain.

Sometimes it looks like silence.

Sometimes it looks like sharing your fries.

Sometimes it looks like holding hands under the school desk while pretending you're strangers.

And sometimes it hurts.

But even that is a form of staying.

I've written this in stolen moments. In the spaces between my breakdowns.

In the cracks of my studies. In the soft bruises of friendships that outgrew their names.

I've written this like I breathe—desperately.

Because writing has always been my way of surviving emotions too big for my body.

Celestial Romanticism isn't a genre. It's a rebellion.

A softness that refuses to be silenced.

It's writing "I love you" with your eyes, even when your mouth forgets how to speak.

It's finding metaphors in her silence, finding poetry in his hoodie, finding a universe in a shared glance.

It's loving in a language only the moon understands.

To the moon—you already know.

You've seen it all. My tears. My hopes. My half-written poems. You've never left.

You stayed when I couldn't even stay with myself.

Thank you.

To my trio—this book is ours.

This isn't my success; this is our grief. Our growth. Our eternity.

You gave me something to believe in again. Something worth writing for.

To the reader—

If you've ever been too emotional, too intense, too quiet, too much—

Then this is yours too.

If you've ever looked at someone and felt a poem write itself inside your ribs—this is yours.

If you've ever cried at 2AM for a reason even you didn't understand—this is yours.

This book is my soul printed in a language called pain.

But pain, in its own way, is just proof of how much we care.

So don't be afraid to feel everything.

Don't be afraid to underline lines that feel like scars.

Don't be afraid to cry.

I cried while writing this too.

It's just us writers and poets against the world. Why does melancholy never leave me? Why am I always sad by the absence of the moon? Why am I always hurt? Why do I always overthink? Why am I always bothered? Just because I'm a writer? Just because I'm a poet? Just because I'm an author? Just because I'm a dreamer? Is that the curse you have to take to become a writer?

It's also something I needed.

Because there were nights when I couldn't sleep without writing, and days when writing felt like dragging my own shadow across the floor.

I would sit with my pen and ask the sky for a sentence. Just one sentence that didn't sound like every other heartbreak I've ever known.

But that's the thing with emotions—they don't leave quietly. They keep knocking, gently, consistently, until you answer.

There were pages I tore out because they sounded too hopeful. And others I left in because they sounded exactly like the way it feels to miss someone who is still alive but not with you anymore.

I never wanted perfection—I only wanted truth.

And truth, for me, has always lived in the in-between.

Between reality and dreams. Between goodbye and almost. Between the version of myself I show the world and the one who writes at 4:44 AM while everyone else is asleep.

This book lives in that space.

It also lives in the classroom corner where I first saw someone looking at someone else like they were made of stars.

It lives in the backseat of an auto, watching the city blur while I pretend I'm not thinking about them.

It lives in the lunch breaks where friendship tasted like shared food and stolen glances.

It lives in the school corridors, where love once walked barefoot and unannounced.

I've changed while writing this.

Not because I grew older, but because I learned that softness is a strength.

That writing isn't just about beautiful lines. It's about honesty. It's about trembling and still writing anyway.

It's about telling the truth even when your voice shakes.

So I let myself be soft here.

I let myself write things I never said aloud.

I let myself be seventeen, and emotional, and hopeful, and tired, and in love with the very idea of love.

And if there's one thing I know, one thing I've learned again and again—

it's that love doesn't die.

It just changes shape.

Becomes letters.

Becomes metaphors.

Becomes us.

And like always—

It starts with the moon and ends with the stars.

With all that aches,

Amish Puri

Seventeen. Soft. Still trying.

Still believing in the kind of love that never leaves.

Bouquet Of Grattitude

How do you thank the world when you've built your entire soul from its pain and poetry?

I don't know how to begin. Not because I lack the words. But because the words keep weeping.

Still, here I am. With hands full of stars and a throat full of thank yous that never learned how to come out quietly.

So, let this be my bouquet of gratitude.

Not of roses. But of moments.

Of people. Of poems. Of presence. Of silence that stayed and absences that taught.

To the Moon,

You were my first editor. My oldest companion. The only one who never left when I started talking to the sky instead of people.

I looked up at you when my pages were blank and my chest was full.

You never judged. You only glowed.

In every book, you're not a metaphor. You're a memory.

Thank you for teaching me that even distance can be a kind of devotion.

To Love,

Thank you for ruining me enough to write.

Thank you for coming unannounced and leaving with all my metaphors.

You never stayed, but somehow, you never left. You lived in my syntax, in my semicolons, in the pauses between poems.

I write best when I ache worst. And you—

You were my ache.

The beautiful kind.

The kind I don't want to heal from.

To Longing,

You are the ache that never asked to be healed.

The slow burn behind my most delicate lines. The reason I write with pauses longer than sentences.

You are not pain. You are the sweetness that pain leaves behind when it decides to stay a little longer.

In every moonrise, I searched for the eyes that once met mine. Not because I forgot them—but because I couldn't.

You taught me that some loves aren't meant to end. They are meant to echo.

And echo you did.

In every poem, every half-written letter, every story that stopped at almost.

Thank you for teaching me that absence, too, can be romantic.

You made me a writer.

You made every sigh a sonnet.

To Heartbreak,

You were not a villain.

You were a mirror.

You showed me who I was when no one stayed to remind me.

You came like thunder—loud, unapologetic, and final. But in the silence after you left, I heard my own voice for the first time.

You shattered things, yes. But you also cleared space for art to grow.

Thank you for the way you taught me to survive.

For turning my silence into a stage.

For making my heart tender enough to recognize beauty in brokenness.

And thank you—

For not staying forever.

Because even poets deserve peace.

To Reunion,

You walked in like a prayer answered at the wrong hour—unexpected, holy, and aching.

You weren't loud. You were soft. You reminded me that love returns in whispers, not in announcements.

You didn't apologize for being late. You just held my hand like it never left yours.

Thank you for proving that sometimes, what leaves can come back softer.

Better.

Brighter.

More knowing.

Thank you for showing me that love, when it chooses to return, is never the same—

But always worth the wait.

You are the comma after heartbreak.

The line after the final full stop.

You are poetry's favorite plot twist.

To My Best Friend,

You are the ink behind this book.

Your love story reminded me that real things still exist. That love isn't always loud — sometimes it's just two people holding space for each other, without asking, without leaving.

Thank you for letting me witness your tenderness.

For trusting me with your real.

This book carries your shadow, your sigh, your sparkle.

And I hope you see yourself between the stanzas — not as a character, but as the pulse that made the page breathe.

    To The Ones Who Left,

I don't curse you. I don't hate you.

I thank you.

Because had you stayed, I might've never picked up a pen.

It was your leaving that birthed this version of me. The one who writes in the margins. The one who finds God in metaphors. The one who builds empires from abandonment.

You taught me that not all disappearances are disasters.

Some are directions.

    To Celestial Romanticism,

You are my genre. My invention. My rebellion.

When the world said "stop feeling so much," you said, "feel more."

When they laughed at how deeply I loved, how easily I cried, how desperately I held onto meaning, you whispered—

"This is exactly what makes you whole."

You gave me permission to be soft in a world that rewards hardness.

You gave me poetry not as an art, but as armor.

You gave me a home in the stars, even when the earth turned cold.

To My Books,

Thank you for carrying my grief. For holding my rage gently. For not complaining when I rewrote you ten times, then erased you again.

You weren't easy births. You were long, painful, and full of self-doubt.

But you became constellations.

And now, strangers find themselves in your wounds.

That's magic.

To My Reader,

Yes, you.

You who picked this book up thinking it would be soft and found yourself crying by page three.

You who reread lines and whispered "that's me" under your breath.

You who stayed.

Thank you for being the kind of person who believes that emotions are not weaknesses, but windows.

Thank you for letting my pain hold your hand.

Thank you for making this genre feel like home.

To My Inner Child,

I see you.

The boy who cried quietly because he didn't know where else to put his feelings.

The boy who thought he was "too much."

The boy who wrote poems on the back of math sheets and hid them from the world.

Look what you've made now.

You didn't just survive — you created a galaxy.

> To Pain,

Thank you for not killing me.

You came dressed as loss, as betrayal, as loneliness.

But beneath it all, you came with purpose.

You turned me into a writer.

You carved out space for poetry to bloom.

I owe every stanza to you.

> To Faith,

I don't talk about you much.

But you've always been in the background.

A quiet breath. A flicker. A reason to believe that even if I have nothing else, I still have words.

And words are enough.

> To The Future Me,

I hope you're still soft.

Still emotional.

Still believing that love matters more than logic.

Still writing about the moon like she's listening.

Still not afraid to cry on paper.

> And finally…

To the One I Haven't Met Yet,

I don't know your name.

But I know your presence will be a poem I've been trying to write my whole life.

When you come, I'll already have a book waiting for you.

It will be this one.

Thank you.

All of you.

For everything.

For staying. For hurting. For healing. For holding space for this tender, trembling voice of mine.

You made me possible.

And as always,

It starts with the moon and ends with the stars.

Amish Puri

Soft. Grateful. And always writing beneath the cosmos.

Epiphanies Of Forever

"Does anything ever, last forever? "

Forever is not time. It is not the clock. It is not the number of sunrises someone stood by you.

Forever is the way someone looked at you in a crowded hallway.

The way your name sounded in their throat when they weren't trying to be poetic but ended up being a poem anyway.

Forever is how your heart still pauses when you remember that one touch, that one goodbye that never said goodbye.

And yet, it is more than that.

It is the way longing taught me to write.

The way heartbreak didn't destroy me—but redesigned me.

It is how I became a cathedral of unsaid things, stained with love letters I never had the courage to send.

Some people think forever is a promise.

But I've come to believe it's a feeling.

A glance, a silence, a held breath.

A piece of someone that lives in your poems long after they stopped living in your life.

And maybe, just maybe, the things that don't last are the ones that stay with us the longest.

Because in the celestial grammar of the soul, not all commas need closure.

Some stories end in ellipses.

I used to think forever was about who stayed.

But now I know—it

The moon taught me that.

How it keeps shifting, fading, glowing. How it is never constant yet never absent.

Much like the people we love.

Much like the version of ourselves we become in their memory.

And so, I write. Not to preserve them, but to preserve who I was when I loved them.

Because even if the hands let go, the soul remembers. Even if the eyes forget the face, the heart remembers the ache.

Forever lives in that ache. It lives in the lines I underline in books.

In the songs I skip because they remind me too much.

In the stars I whisper names to when no one's listening.

Forever is not infinite.

It is intimate.

The world may move on. People may outgrow each other. But somewhere, in a corner of the universe, the moment still exists—untouched, undamaged, suspended.

I call that corner, Forever.

Let me tell you what I've learned in 17 years, as a boy who loved too much, too hard, too soon:

The ones who leave are not always gone.

The moments that hurt are not always cruel.

The versions of me that broke were also the ones who built this book.

And this book—this very one you're holding—is my forever.

It is filled with epiphanies that don't end. That still arrive. That
breathe through margins, that sigh between semicolons,
that knock at midnight when I mistake loneliness for hunger.
That show up in mirrors when I try to move on,
reminding me I was once loved in ways I did not know how to hold.

This book is not a closure. It is a continuation.
A confession of everything I couldn't say when it mattered.
It is a museum of my silences—
each poem a preserved exhibit of what it meant to feel everything
and still survive.

It is a love letter to the ones who held my hand and let go—
and to the ones who stayed in sentences,
if not in sight.

Sometimes I wonder if they ever think of me when it rains,
if their chest tightens at a scent,
if their fingers hesitate before playing that one old song.
Maybe that's all forever ever was—
not eternal presence,
but mutual hauntings.

There is no grave for memories.
They don't die; they just turn quieter.
They shape-shift into metaphors,
disguise themselves in deja vu,
and curl up in the corners of your new beginnings.

I have carried people through pages who never carried me back.
I have loved like a lighthouse—

shining for ships that never intended to dock.
But I've also learned:
To be the light is a blessing,
even when no one returns.

Some nights, I still ache like it's the first time.
But I no longer beg for healing to be fast.
I've learned that wounds bloom slower than flowers
and sometimes—
hurt is the only proof that it mattered.

So I keep writing.
Because the only forever I truly trust
is the one that bleeds onto paper.

Ink doesn't forget.
Paper doesn't interrupt.
And every word I choose
becomes another way of saying,
I was here. I felt this. It was real.

If this book reaches you,
know that you are not alone.
You are not too much for feeling deeply.
You are not broken for holding on.

You are simply someone
who believed in forever—
and that is not a weakness,
but a miracle.

So when you finish this last page,
don't say goodbye.

Say:

We'll meet again—

in another line,

in another life,

under the same moon

that watched us fall in love with everything we couldn't keep.

Because that, darling,

is how forever returns.

Not with footsteps—

but with echoes.

www.ingramcontent.com/pod-product-compliance
Lightning Source LLC
Chambersburg PA
CBHW062144150726
47991CB00006B/2167